Beijing 1986

北京一九八六年

Beijing 1986
Copyright 2016 by Bob Bovin
Bovin Design HB, Lilla Nygatan 15, Stockholm
All rights reserved. No part of this book may be reproduced
Home page: www.bovin.nu/bob
E-mail: bob@bovin.nu
Print and distribution: CreateSpace an Amazon company

Preface by Birgitta Lindqvist. Translated to Chinese by Alexis Lan.
The calligraphy is by Lili Weil.

ISBN: 978-91-981019-2-8

Beijing 1986

Bob Bovin

Preface

When the People´s Republic of China celebrated its 20th Anniversary in 1969 it was at the height of the "Cultural Revolution". Thousands of Red Guards were standing on Tien An Men square shouting "Long live chairman Mao" brandishing the little red book with Mao´s quotations.

I was at that time, living as a Swedish diplomat in Beijing and was invited to these celebrations in the presence of Mao Tse Dong waving at the masses. Millions of people paraded in his honour.

During my two years in China I was confined to Beijing. There was famine in the country and struggles between political fractions. Young intellectuals were sent out into the countryside to learn from the people.

Beijing 1969 was like a rural town with narrow "hutungs" and small traditional houses. There was not a single private car! The streets were filled with bicycles, horse and donkey carts, trolley buses and a few old lorries. People of all ages were dressed in the same way: green or blue cotton trousers and Mao-jackets. It was a totally uniform society. The schools and factories had red flags, political slogans and pictures of Mao.

There were no dogs, cats or birds to be seen – when you are hungry you eat everything. Women were selling cabbages and spring onions, which was the basic food supply. Many old women had bounded feet and the small children their trousers open for their convenience. In the wintertime houses were warmed by coal. Electricity was scarce and toilets were public.

In 1986, fifteen years after I left China, Bob Bovin visited Beijing. Bob walked around in the city and photographed people and street life. Mao Tse Dong died in 1976 and Beijing, ten years after his death, had slowly started its modernisation thanks to Deng Xiao Ping.

Bob´s photos show that the difference however, is not enormous compared to 1969. The traffic was still dominated by bicycles, carts and buses. But people dress a bit differently and you can see some happy faces.

There are a variety of vegetables and fish to buy and some restaurants serve good meals. The political slogans have been torn down – except the portrait of Mao Tse Dong hanging on Tien An Men. Most roads are not paved and there is still no sewage system, no private toilets – the human faeces from the public toilets were emptied and transported by donkey carts onto the fields used as "human fertilizers".

Bob´s photos from Beijing 1986 are an important historical documentation. "A picture says more than a thousand words".

In 2019 The People´s Republic will be 70 years old. It constitutes a very short period in the 6000 thousand years of Chinese civilisation. But the progress and change of the Chinese society during the last thirty years is more than a revolution. The photos in this unique book will remind you of this evolution into modern China. "The Chinese dream" has come true, as Xi Jin Ping puts it.

Paris 2017   Birgitta Lindqvist/Author

Preface in Chinese

1969年，中华人民共和国庆祝成立20周年之时，也正是文化大革命进行得如火如荼之时。成千上万的的红卫兵站在天安门广场上，挥动记录着毛主席语录的红宝书，高喊着"毛主席万岁"。

那时，我以瑞典外交官的身份居住在中国，我也应邀参加了这个庆典，我亲眼见到毛泽东向人群挥手，数以百万的群众骄傲地游行。

在中国的那两年，我被限制在北京生活，农村正经历着的饥荒和政治隔离，年轻的知识分子被送到农村接受贫下中农的再教育。

1969年的北京就像一个到处都是狭窄的胡同和充斥着的中式传统建筑的大农村，满大街甚至找不到一辆私有汽车！马路上满是自行车，马车，驴车，无轨电车和厢式货车。
无论男女老少都穿着同样风格的服装：绿色或蓝色的裤子和中山装，那真是一个完全制服化的社会。学校，工厂到处挂满红旗，政治标语和毛的照片。

几乎从来看不到狗，猫或者鸟——因为饥饿会让你吃得下任何东西。
女人们兜售着卷心菜和大葱，这是最基本的食物供应。
很多年老的妇女有着裹足的小脚，小孩子们穿着方便便溺的开裆裤，冬天人们烧煤取暖，电力供应不足，厕所也都是公用的。

1986年，是我离开中国的第15年，鲍勃·博文来到北京。他行走于大街小巷，用相机记录下那里的人和街头生活。北京，在毛泽东1976年去世后第十年，终于在邓小平的带领下，缓步走向现代化。

从鲍勃的照片中我能看出，1986和1965的中国没有什么巨大的变化——
交通主要还是自行车，马车和巴士，但是人们的着装已经显露出不同的风格，而且你能看到洋溢着幸福的脸庞。市场上能买到的蔬菜和鱼的种类越来越多，餐厅也真正开始提供美味的菜肴，政治标语被撤走——
除了天安门城楼上毛泽东的照片，大多数的道路没有铺砌，没有污水处理系统，人们依然是去公共厕所方便，这样排泄物就由驴车带走到田地里作为"家肥"。

鲍勃1986年在北京拍摄的照片是珍贵的历史记录——一眼胜千言。

2019年，中华人民共和国将成立70周年，它只是这个6000年文明的一小段，但是近三十年来，中国社会所经历的改变和取得的成就远不是一次革命所能给予的。这本影集中的照片会让你看到现代中国的变迁，习近平所说的"中国梦"已经实现。

碧姬泰

Beijing in 1986 is just in the beginning of the industrial revolution. A city showing signs from more than 300 years of living standard. The tourism and the influence from the modern life of the west is about to change that, as can be seen in these photographs.

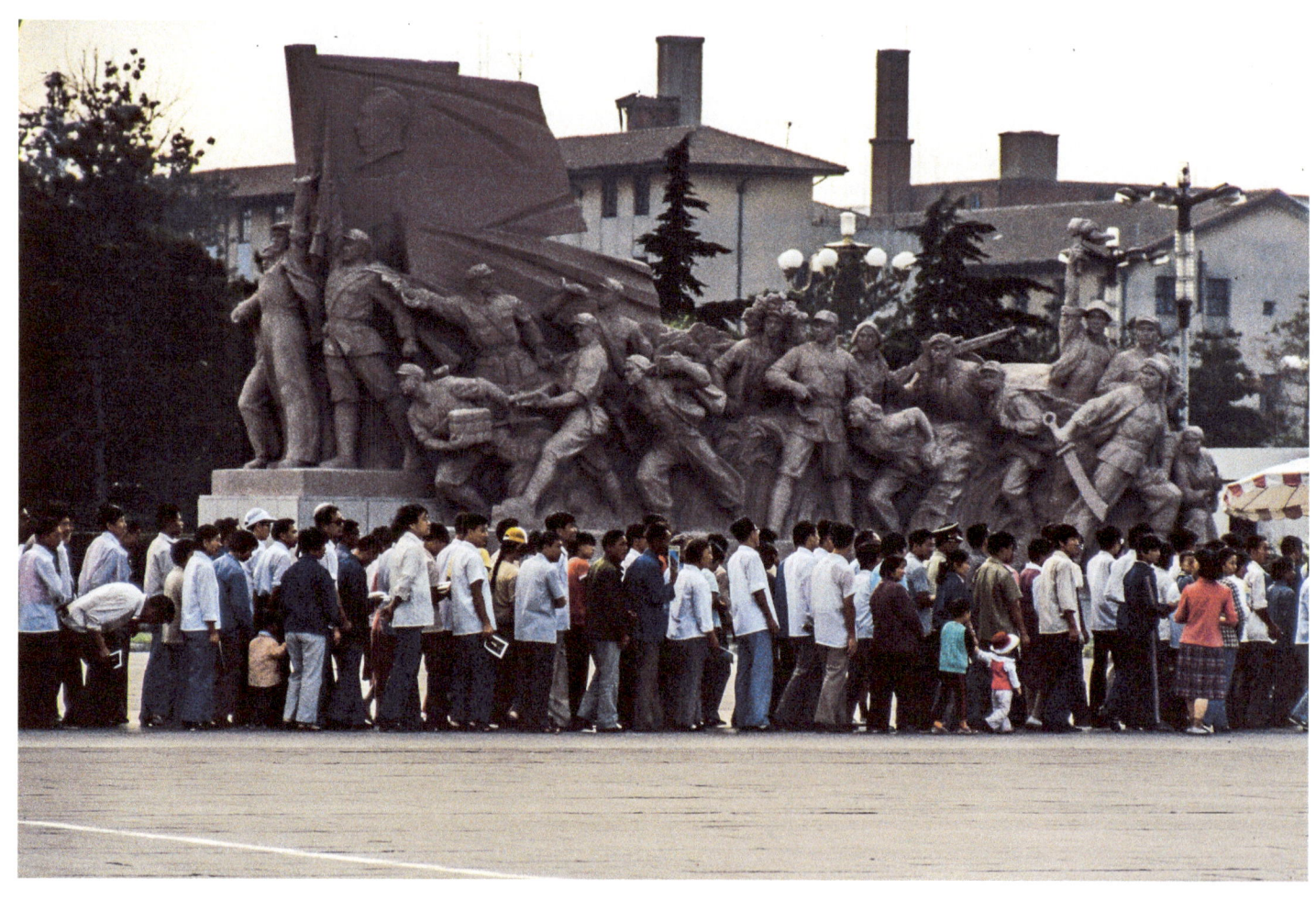

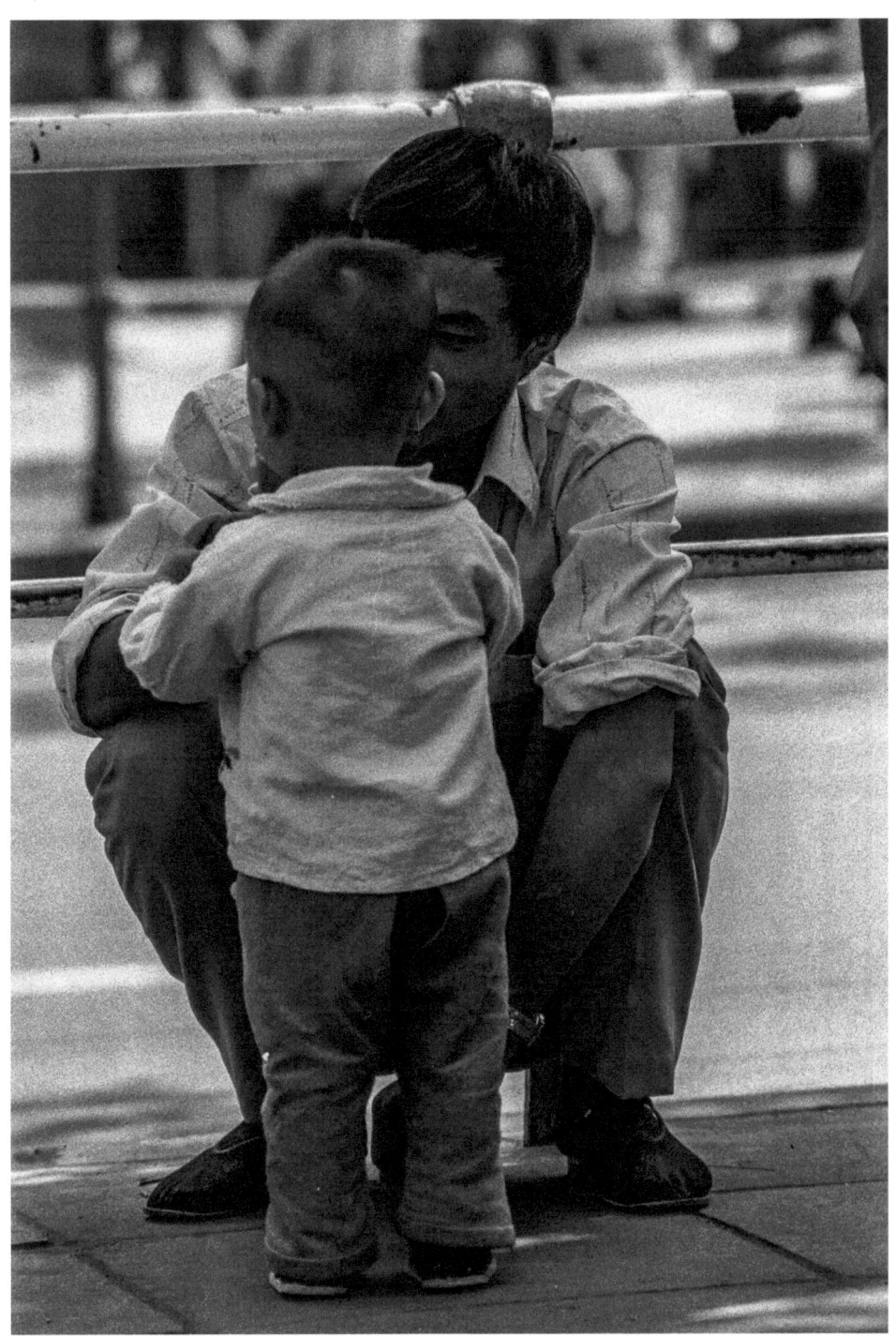

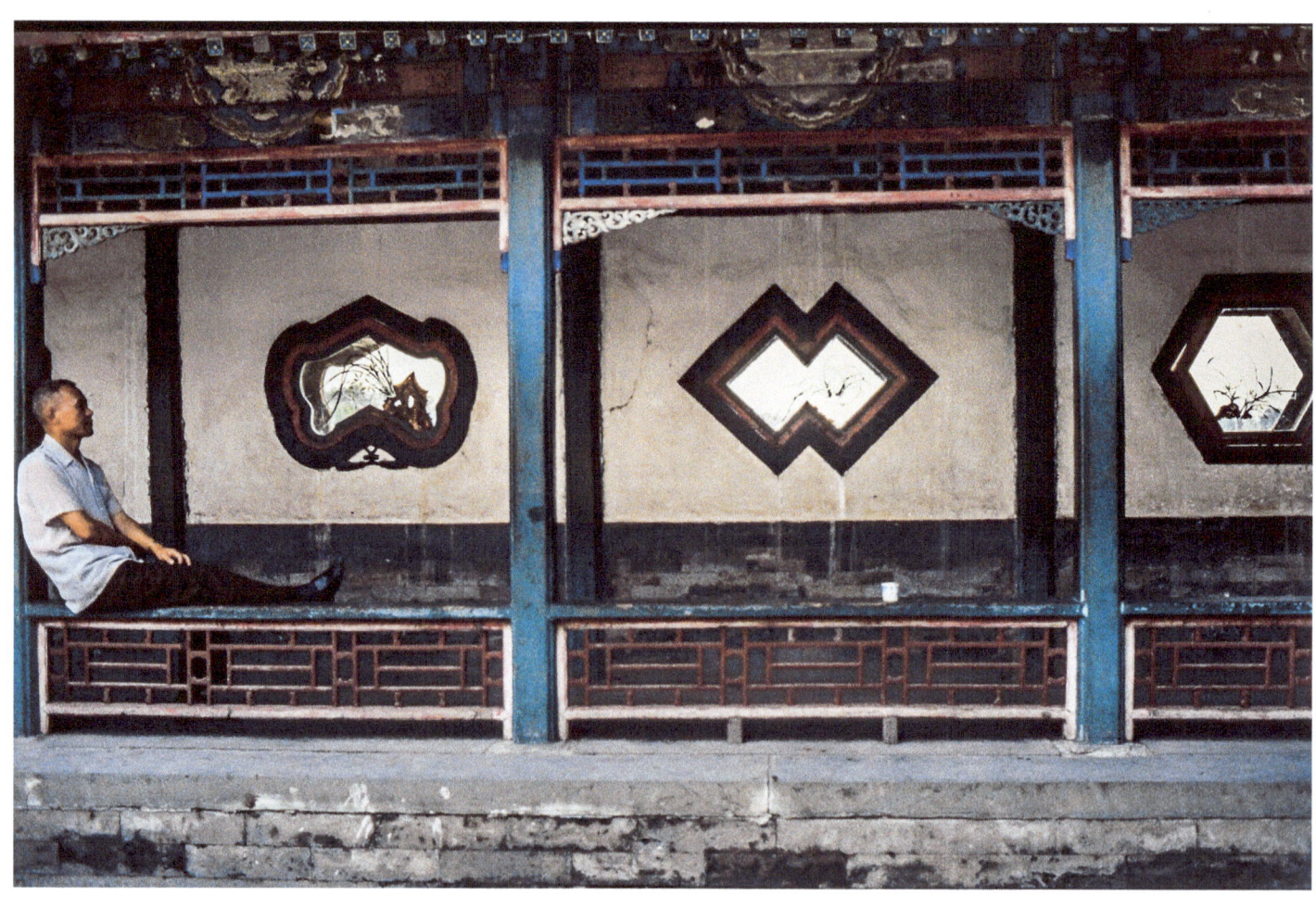

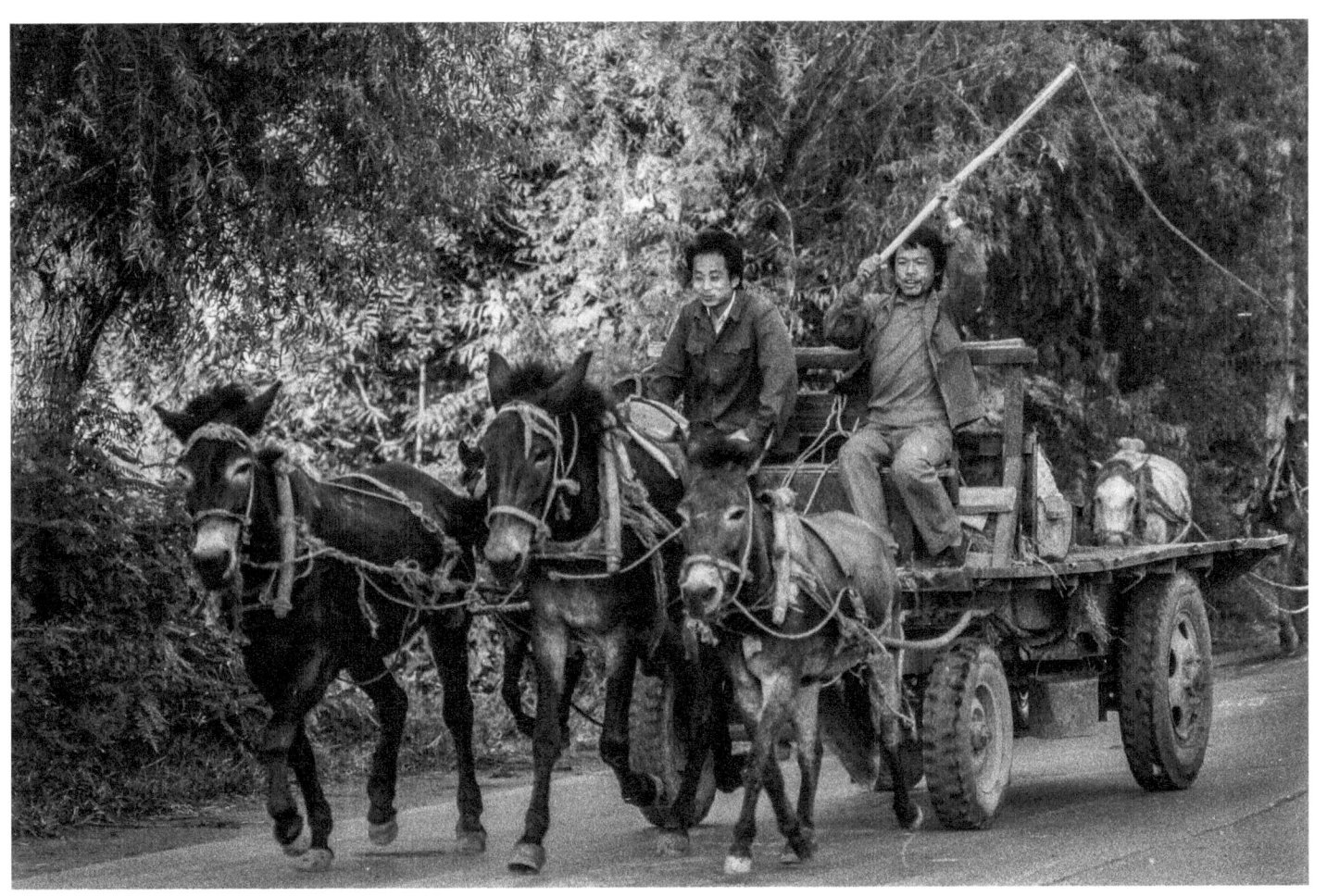

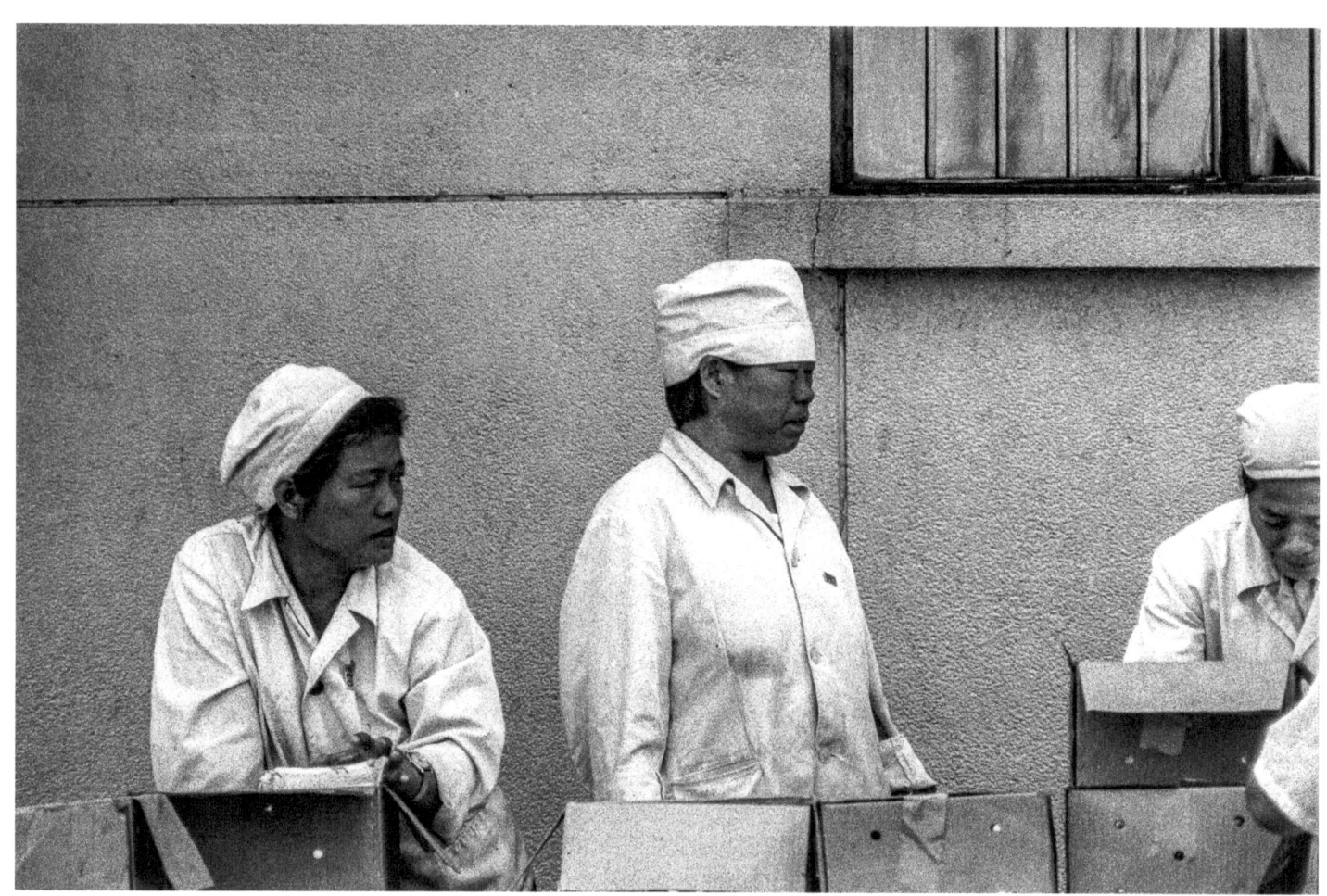

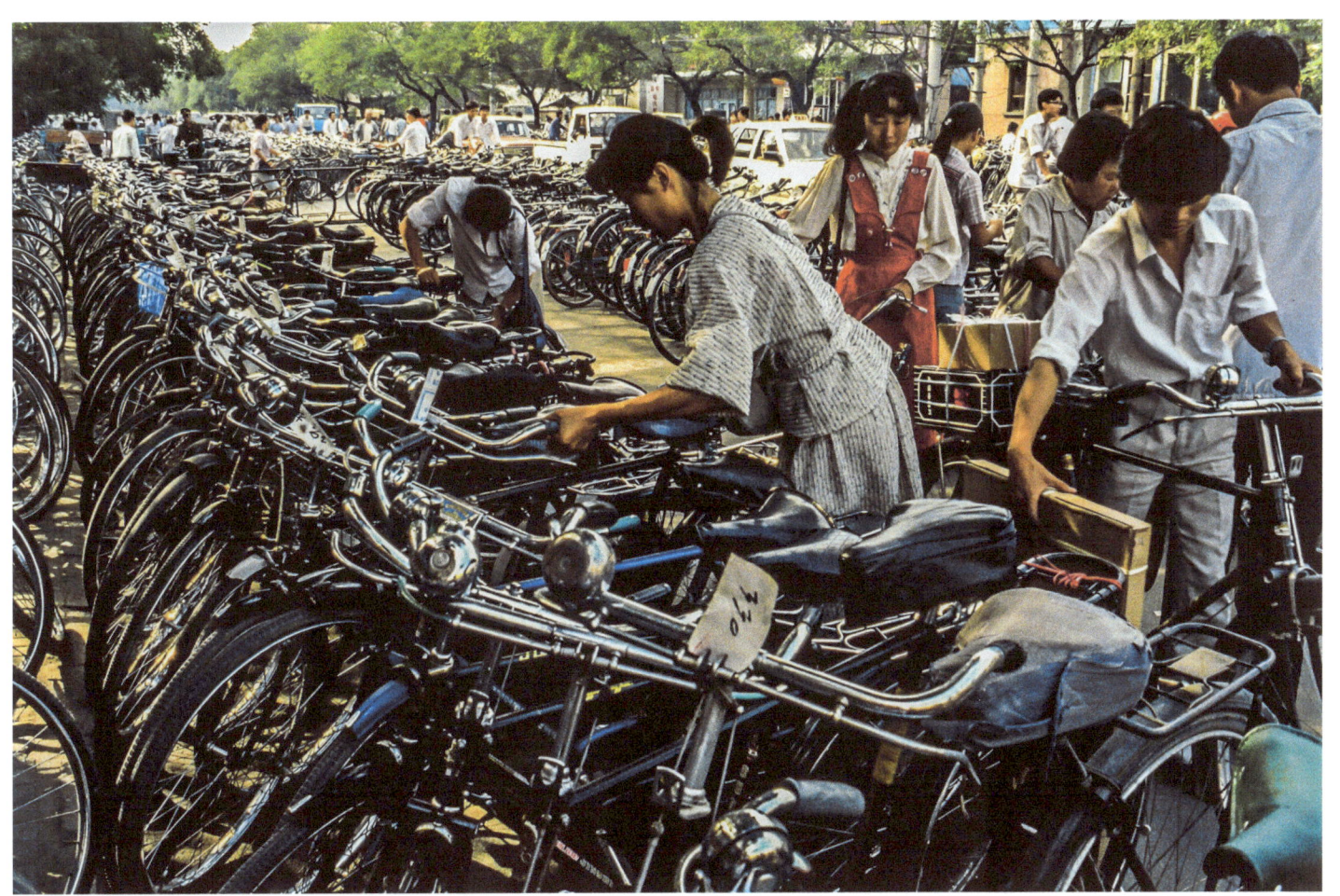

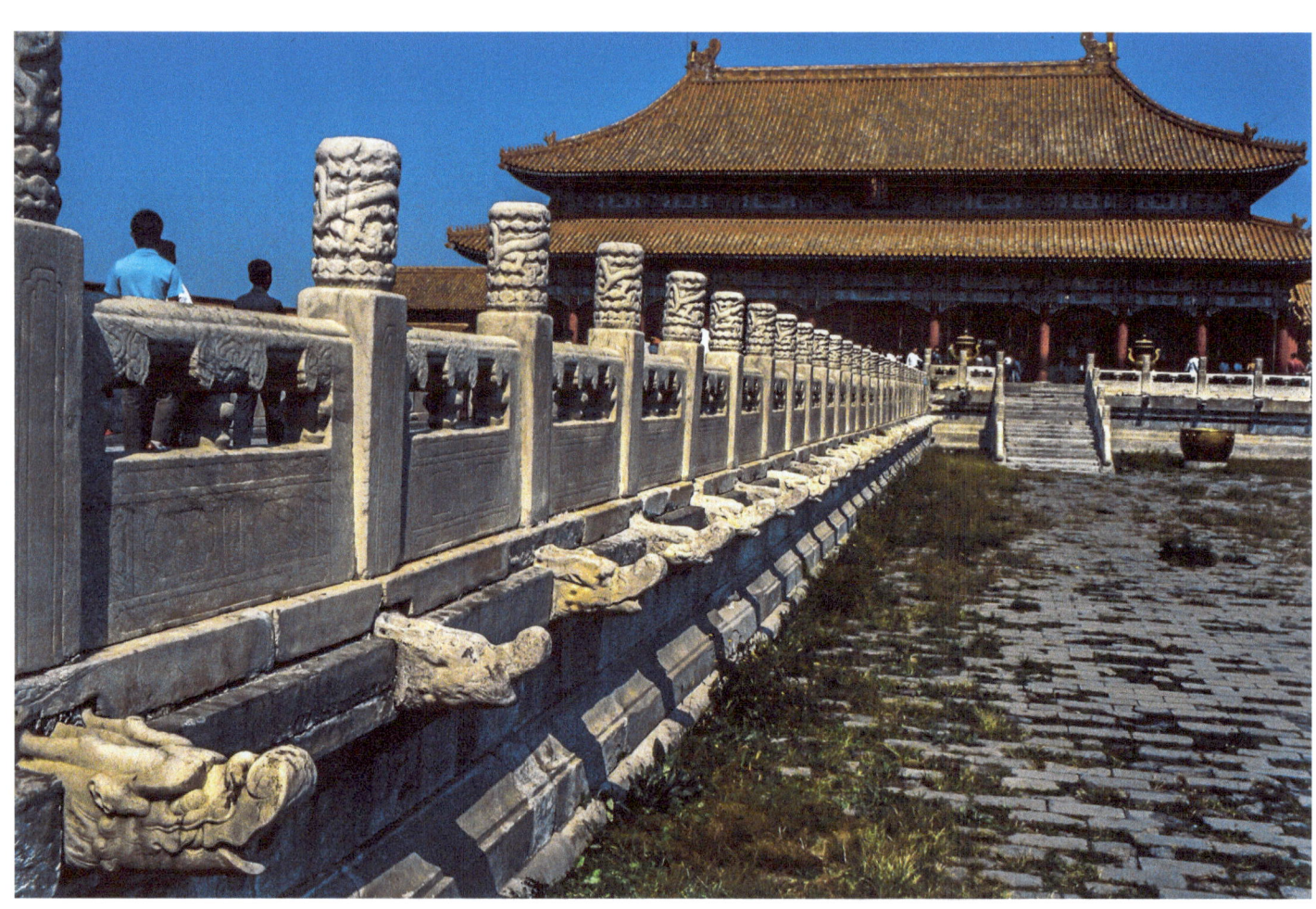

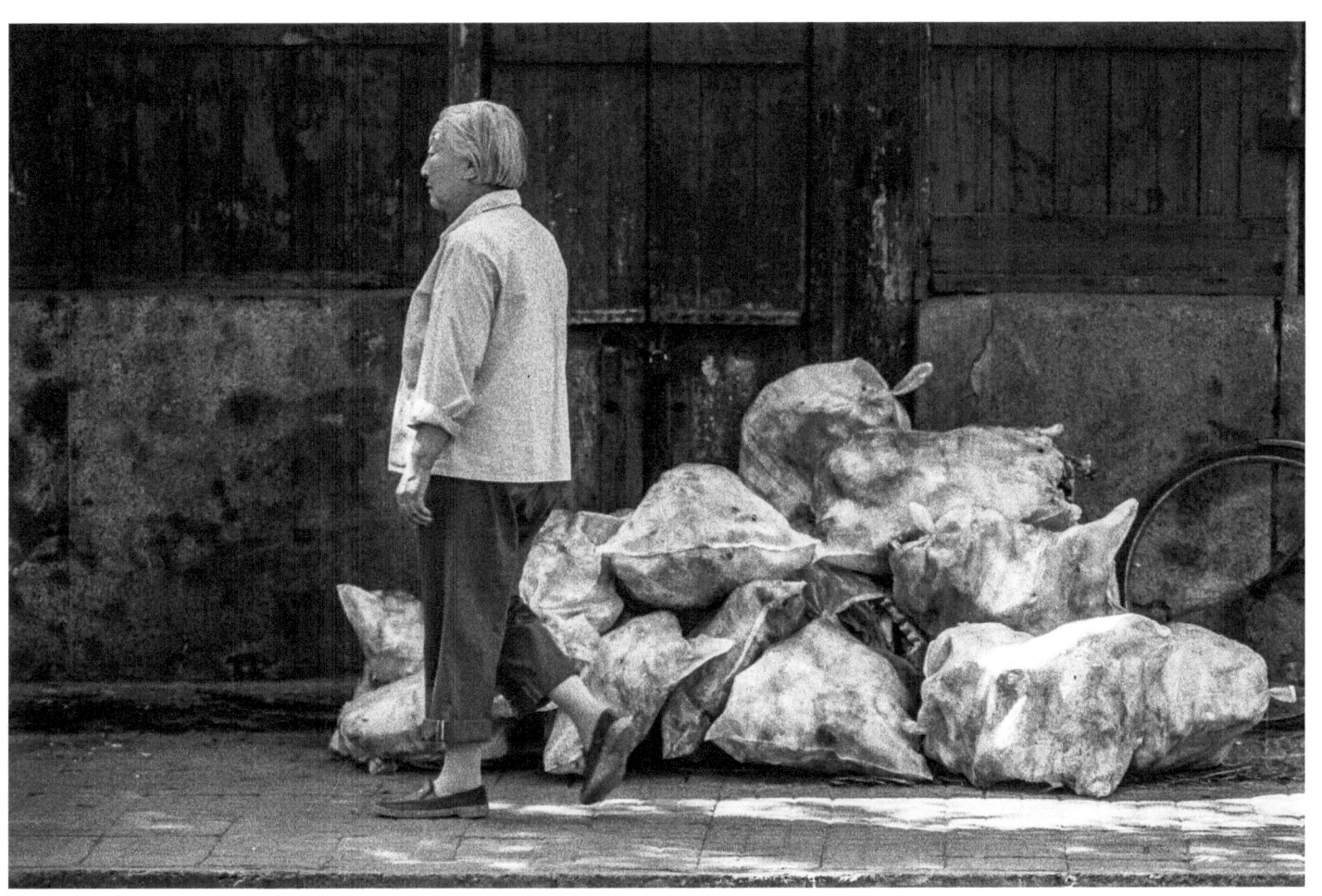

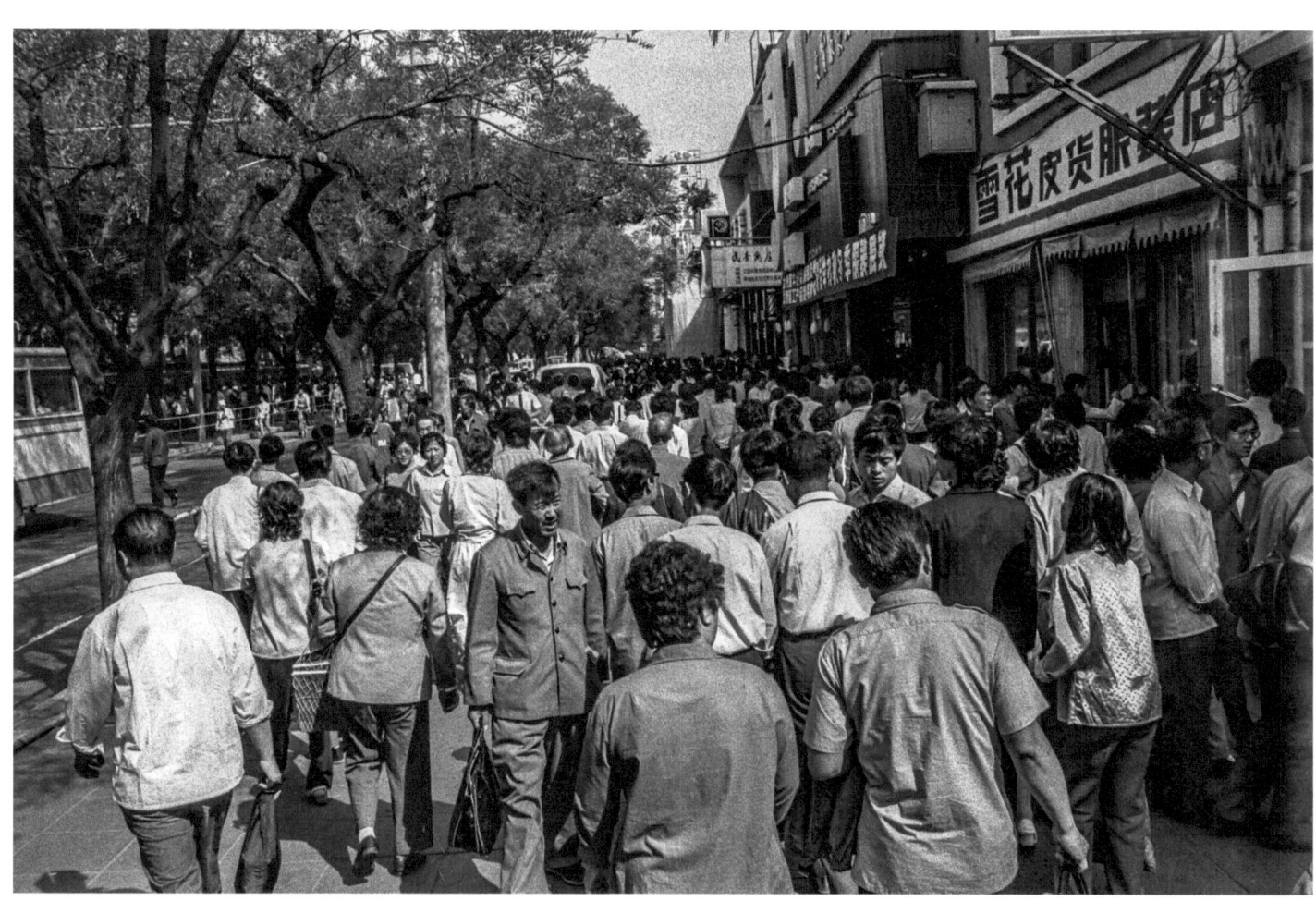

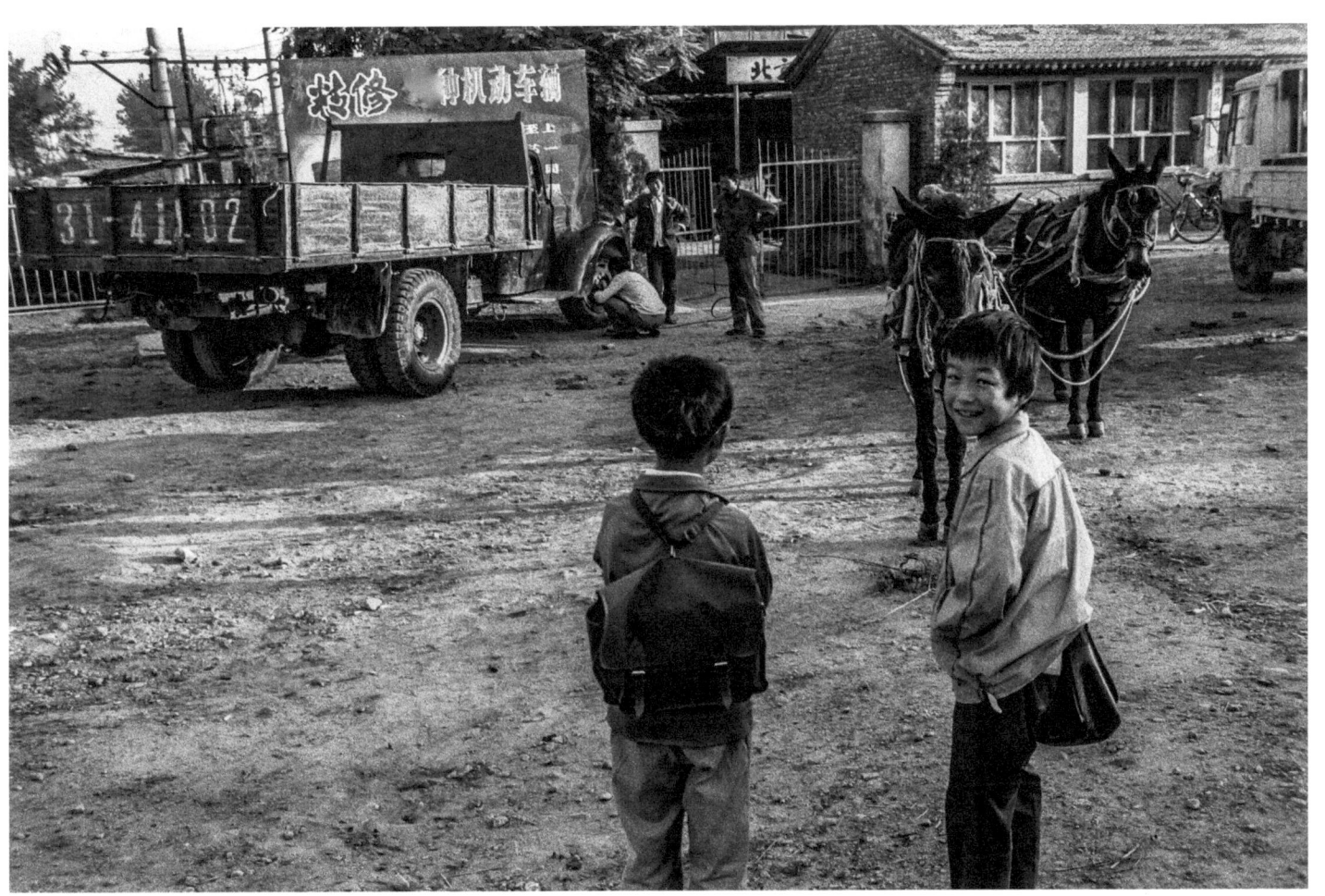

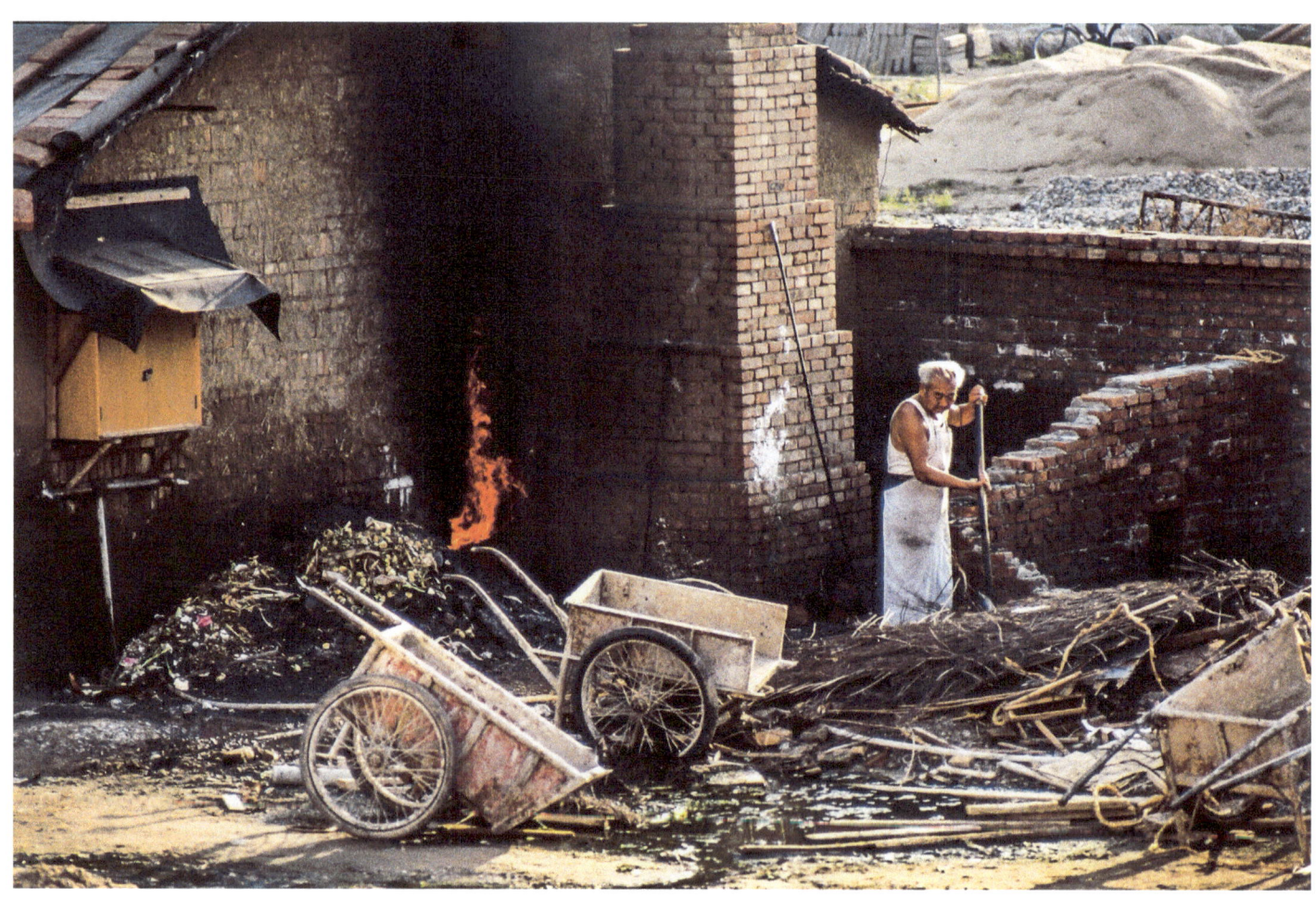

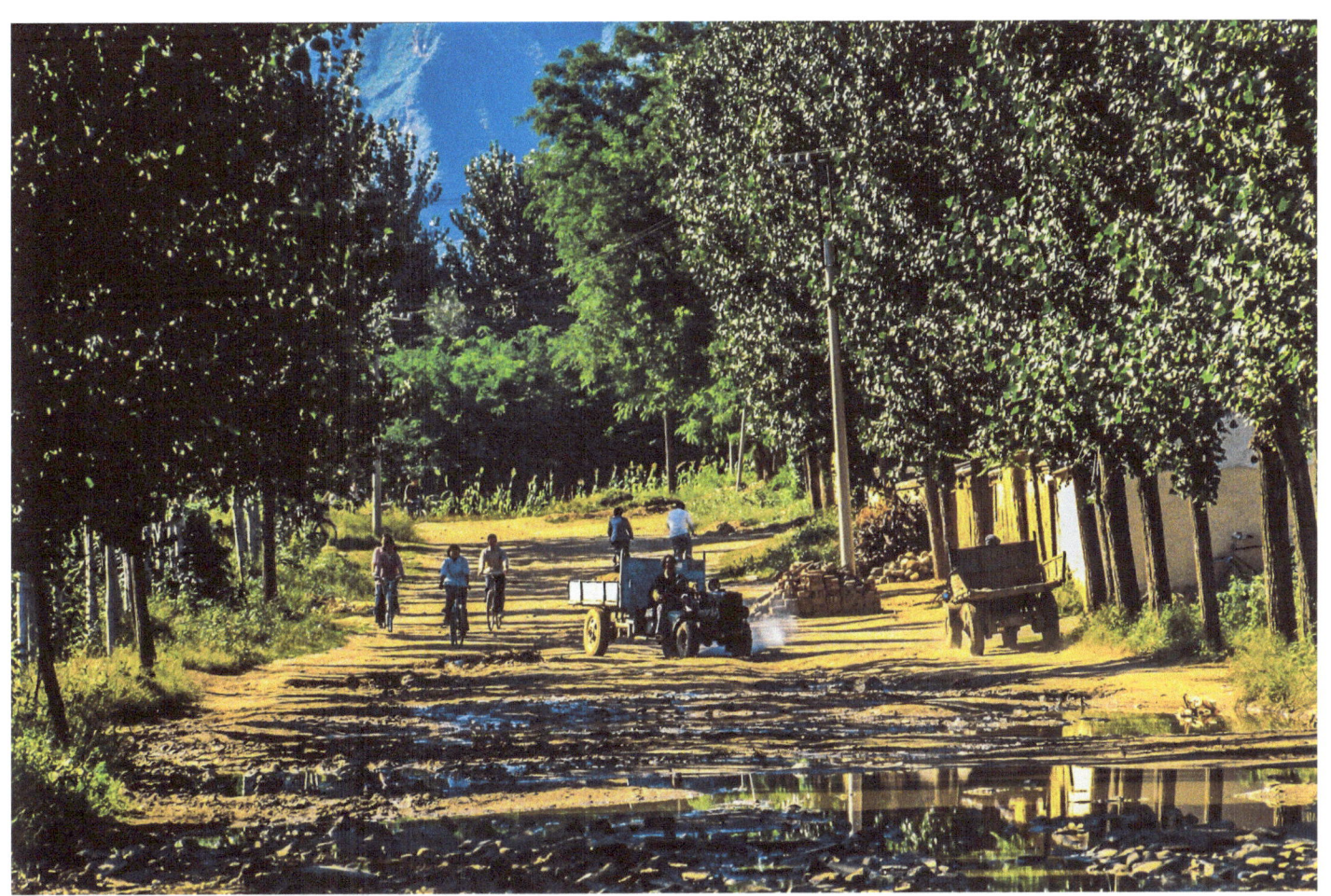

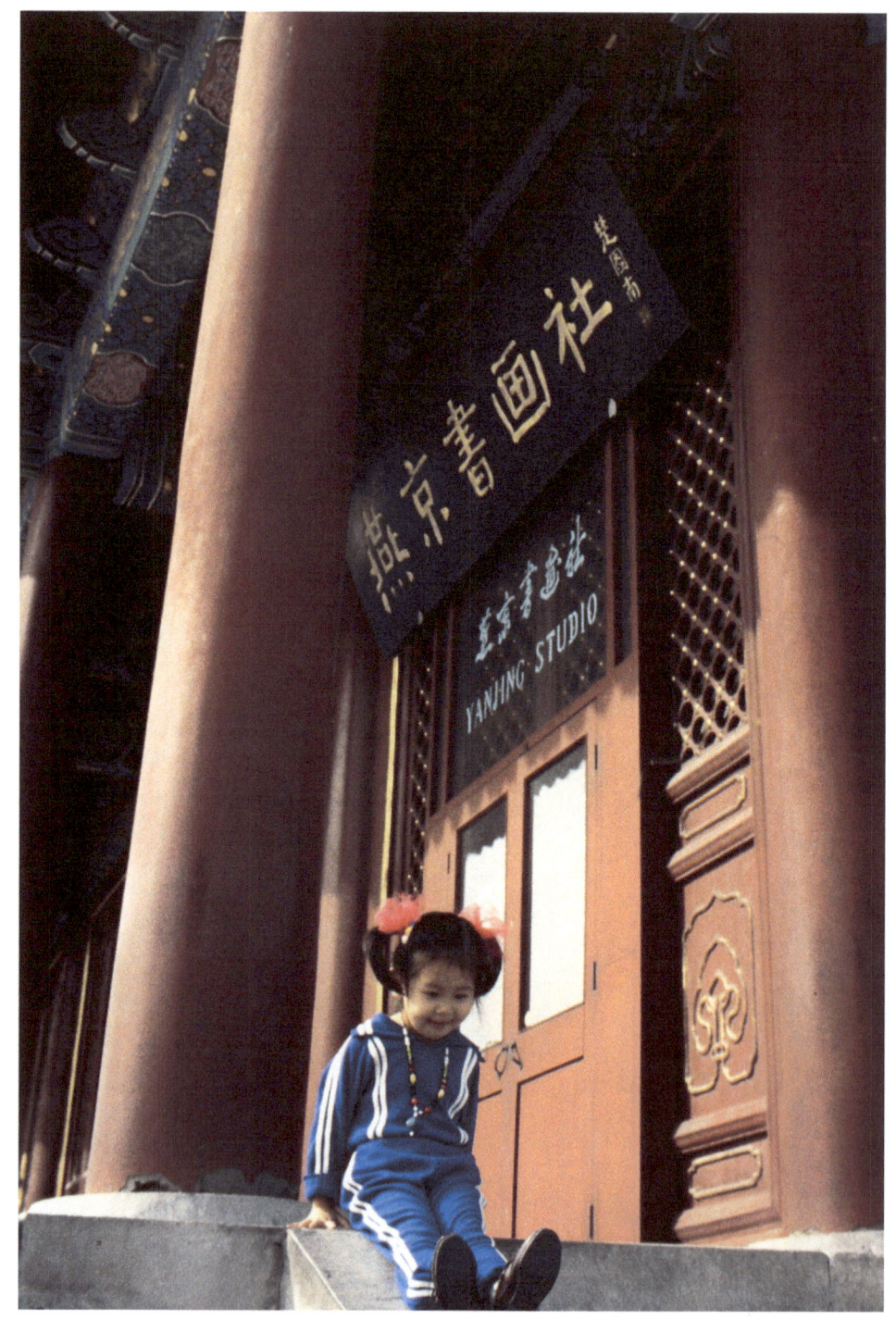

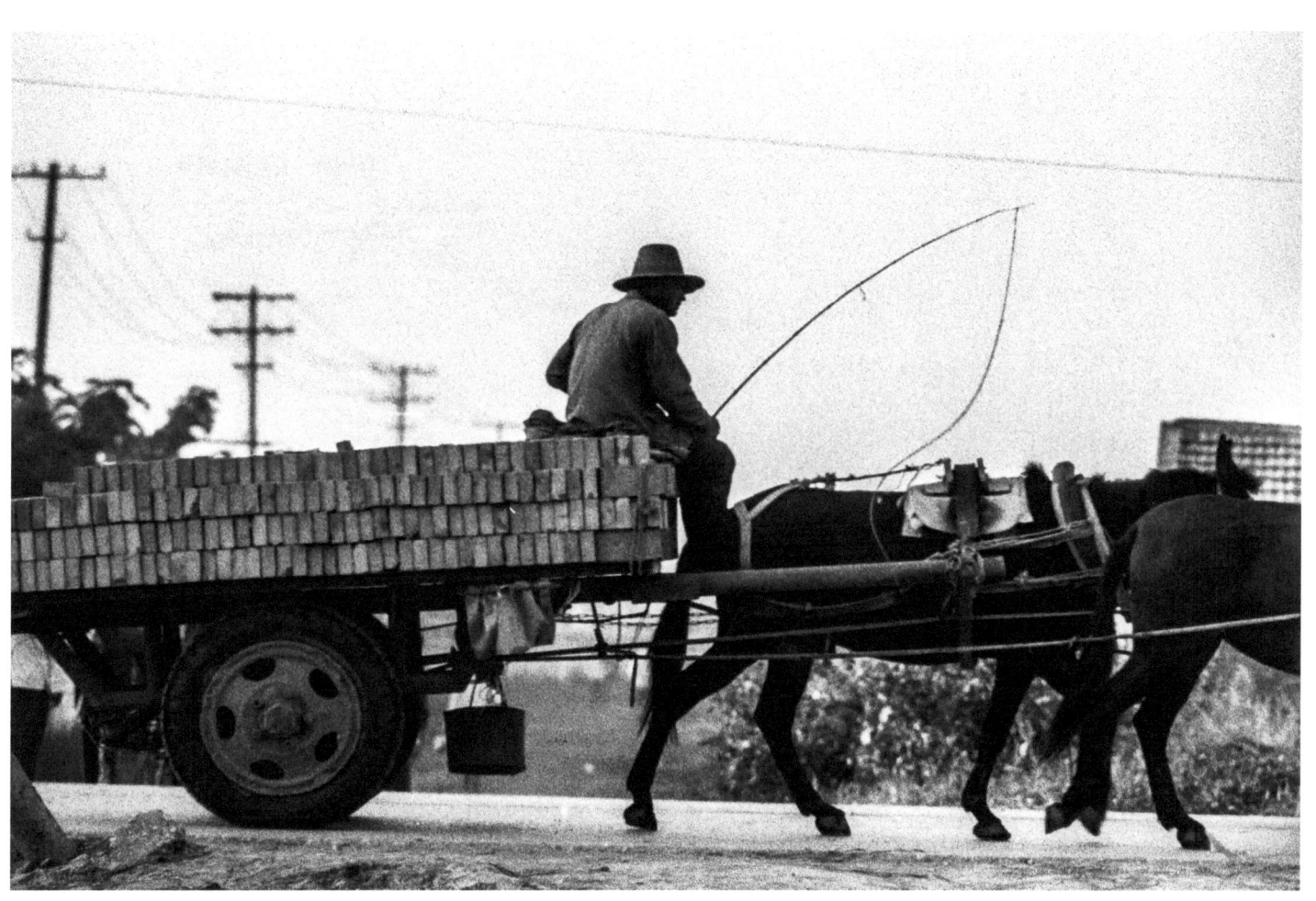

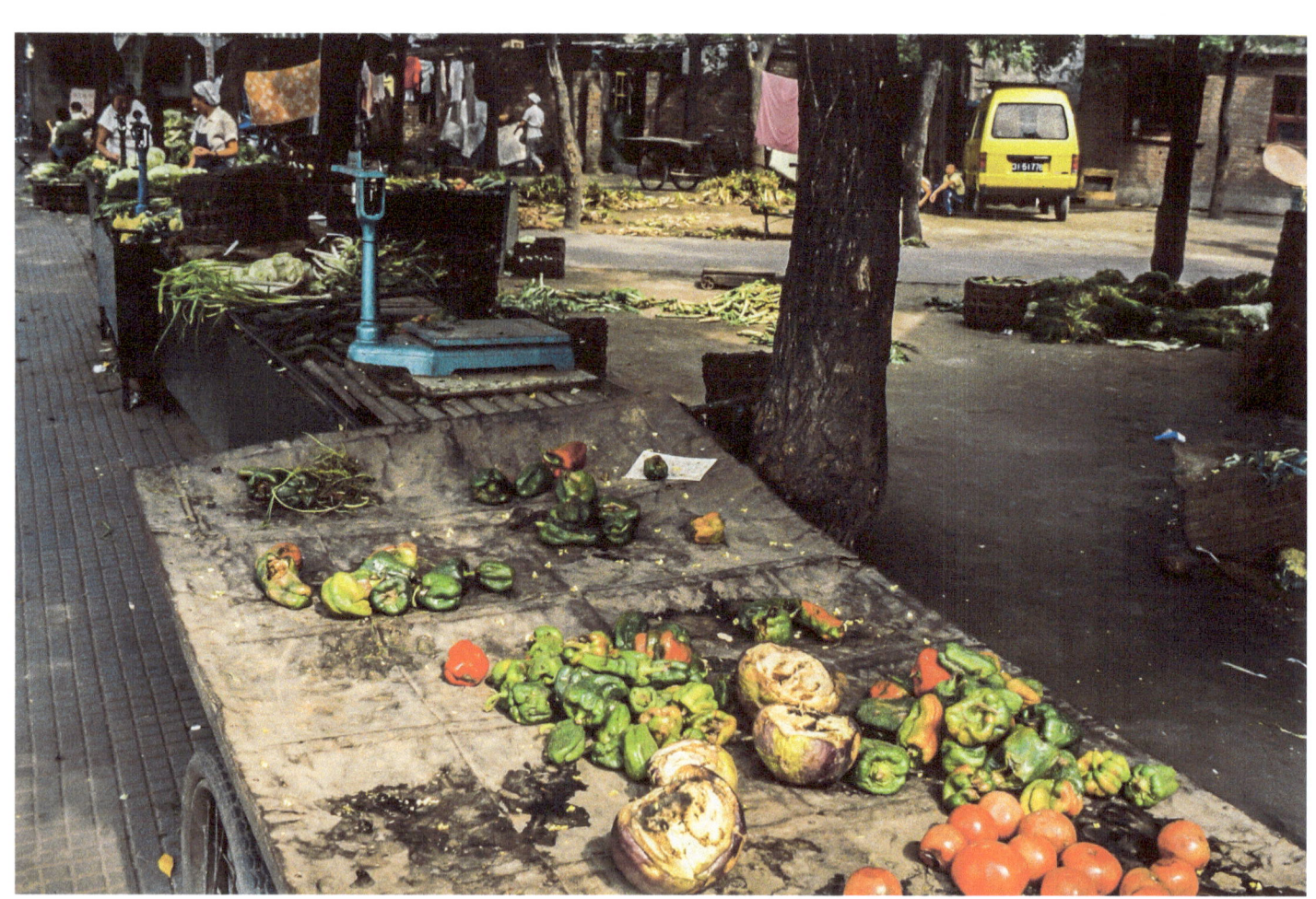

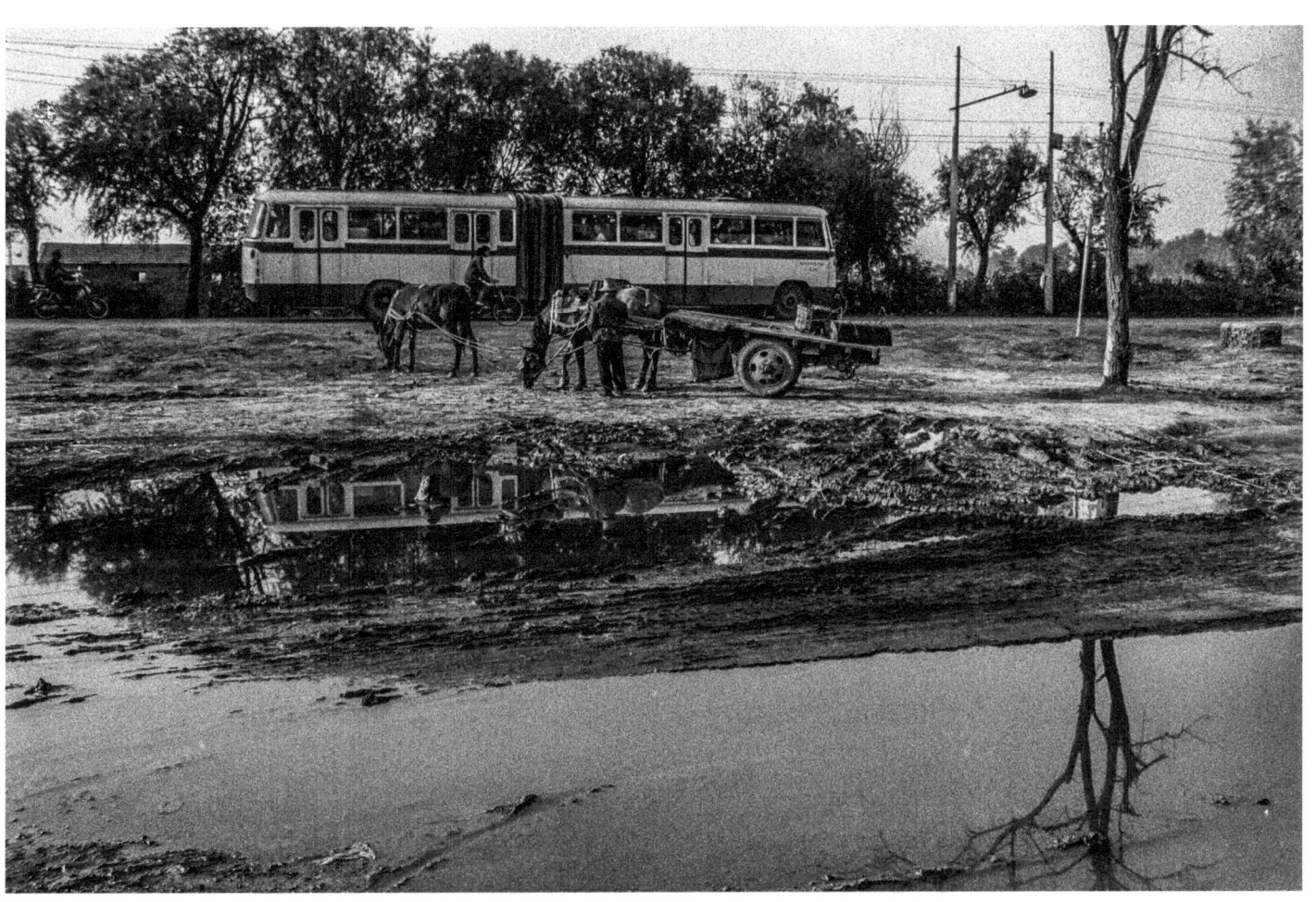

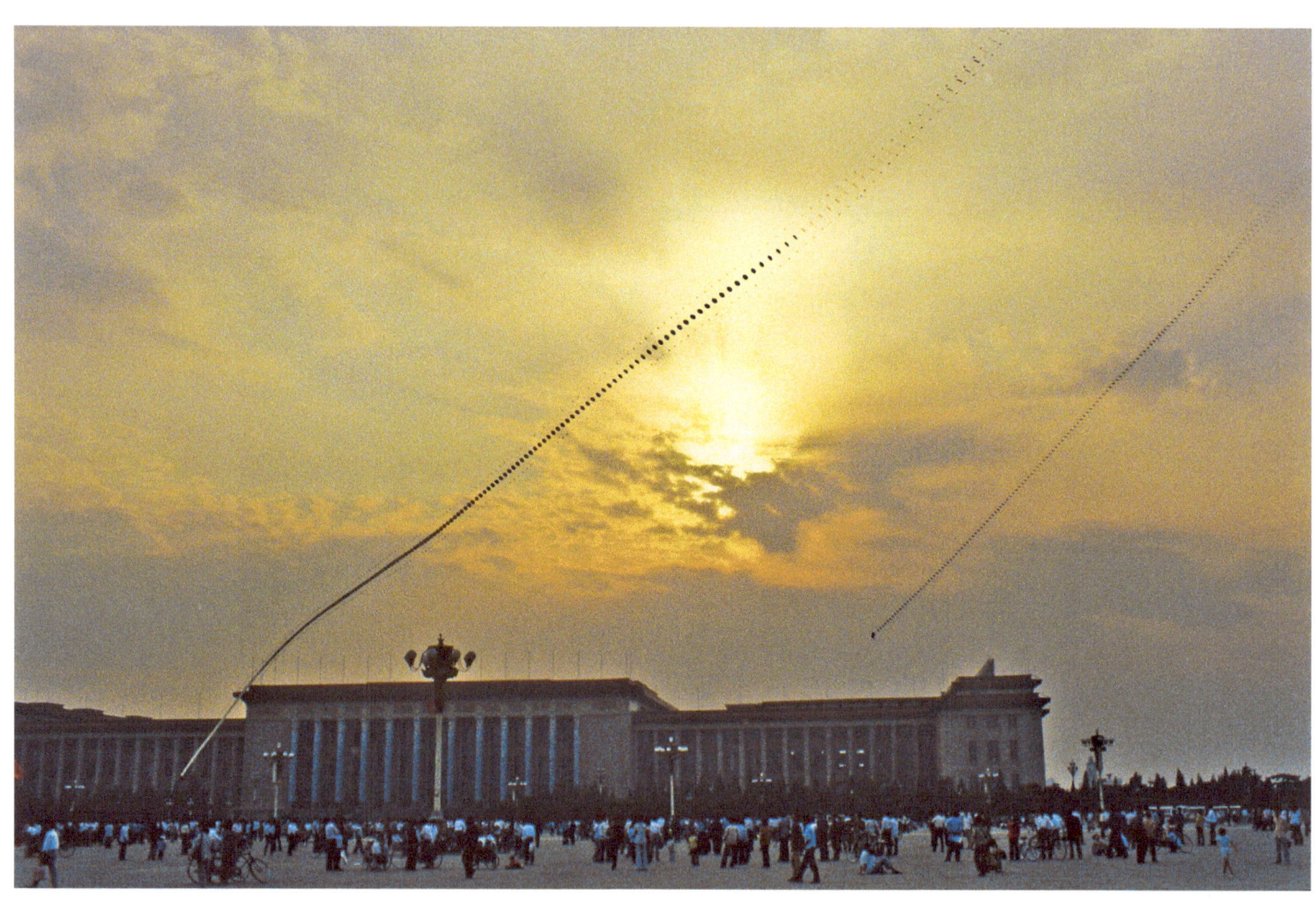

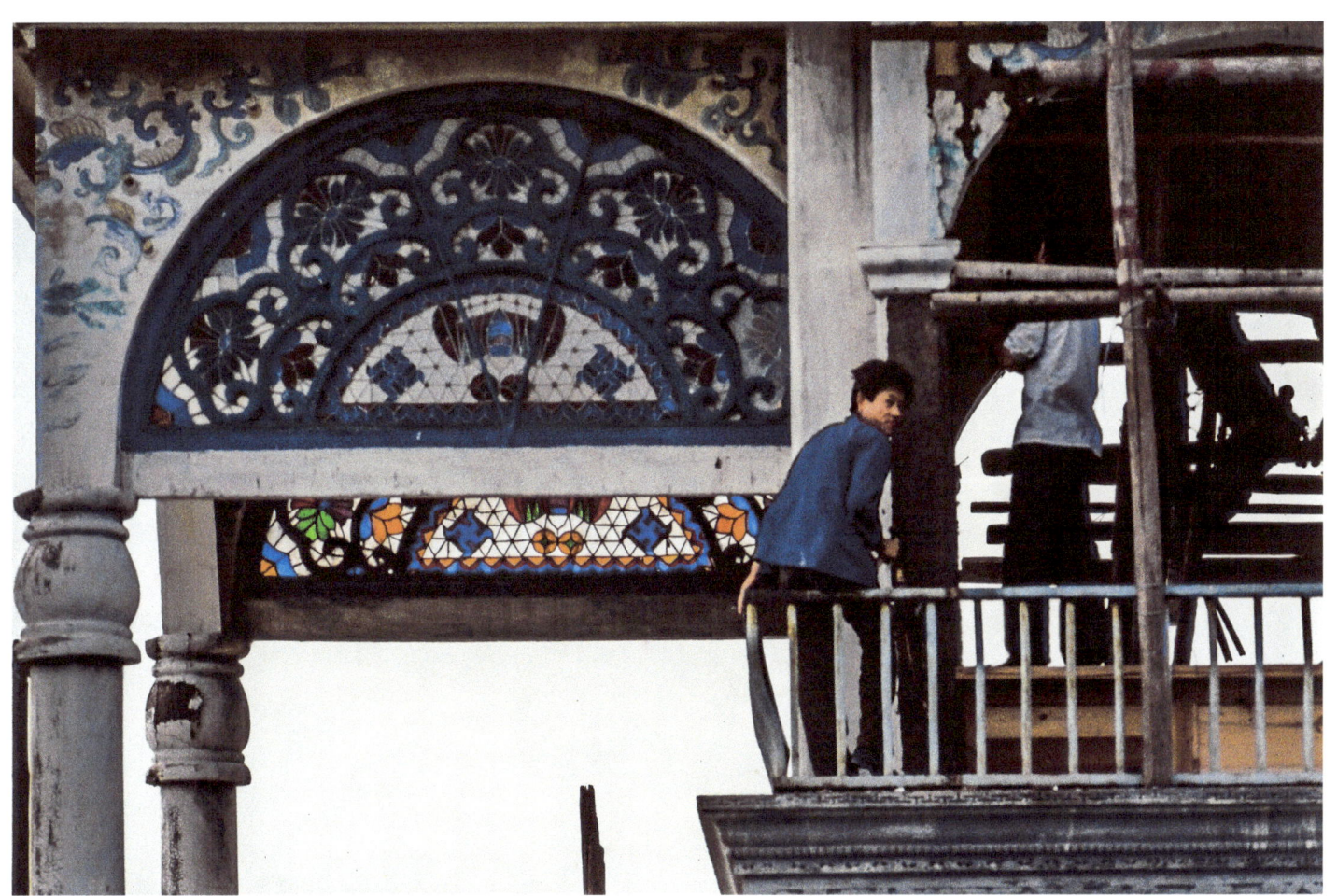

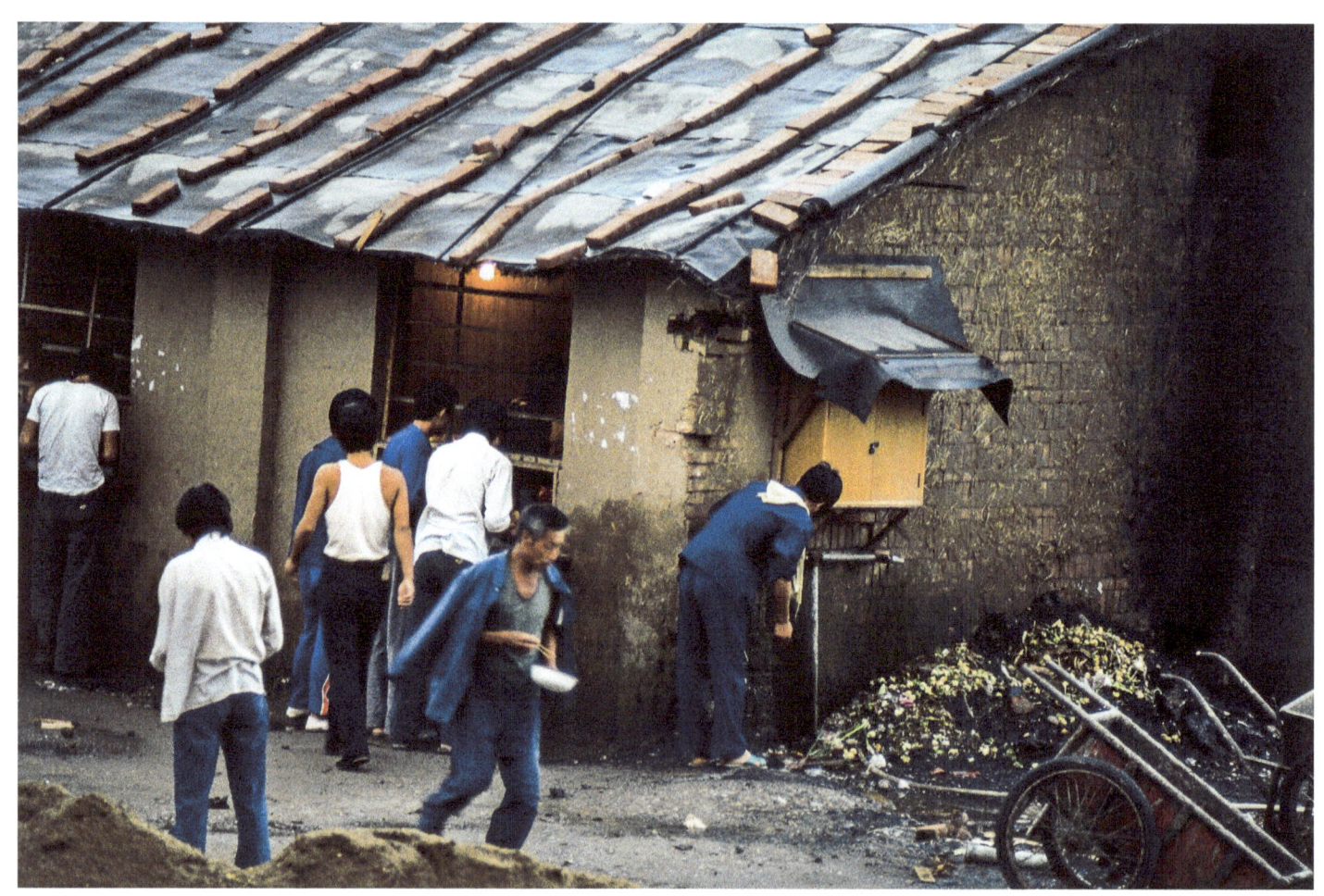

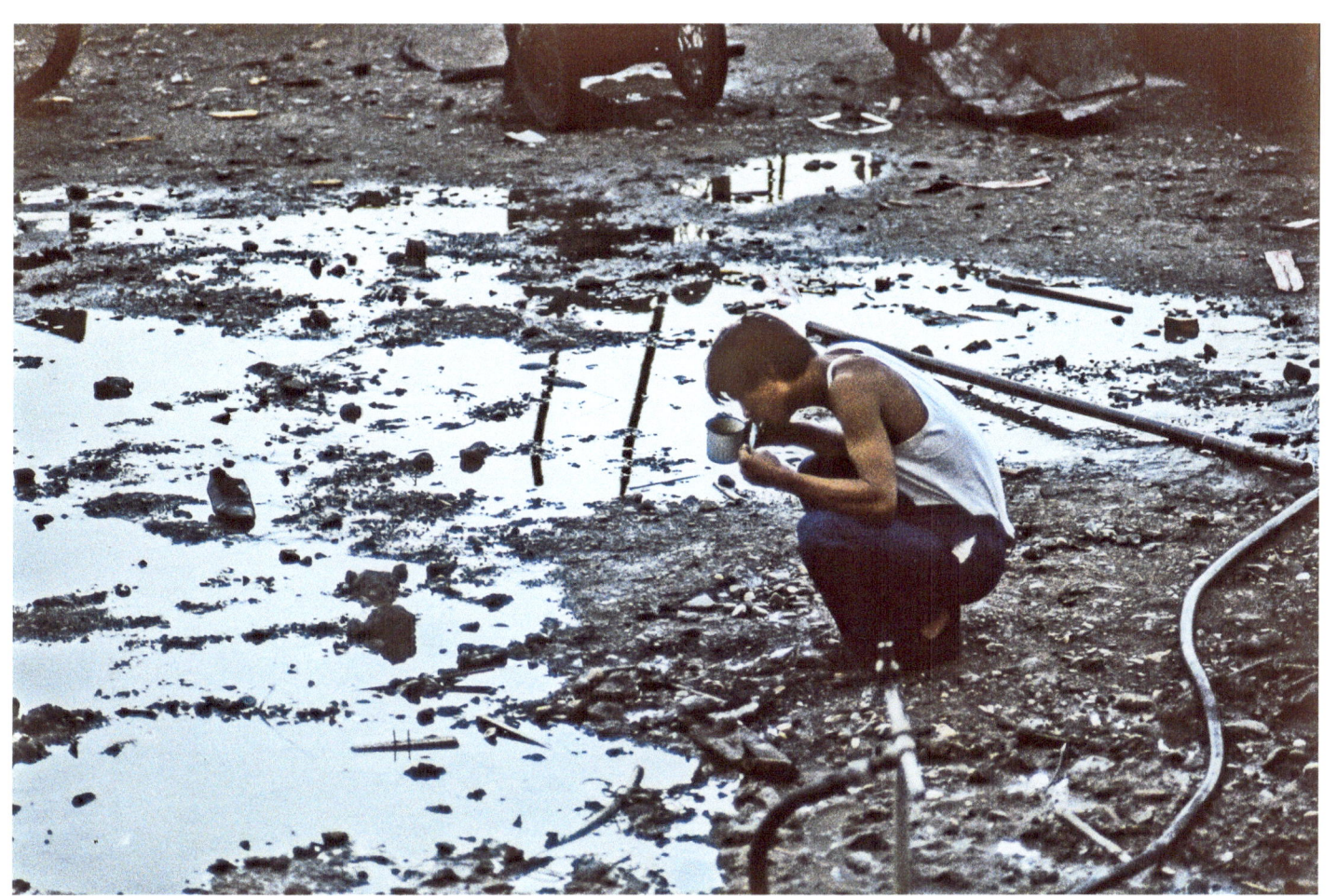

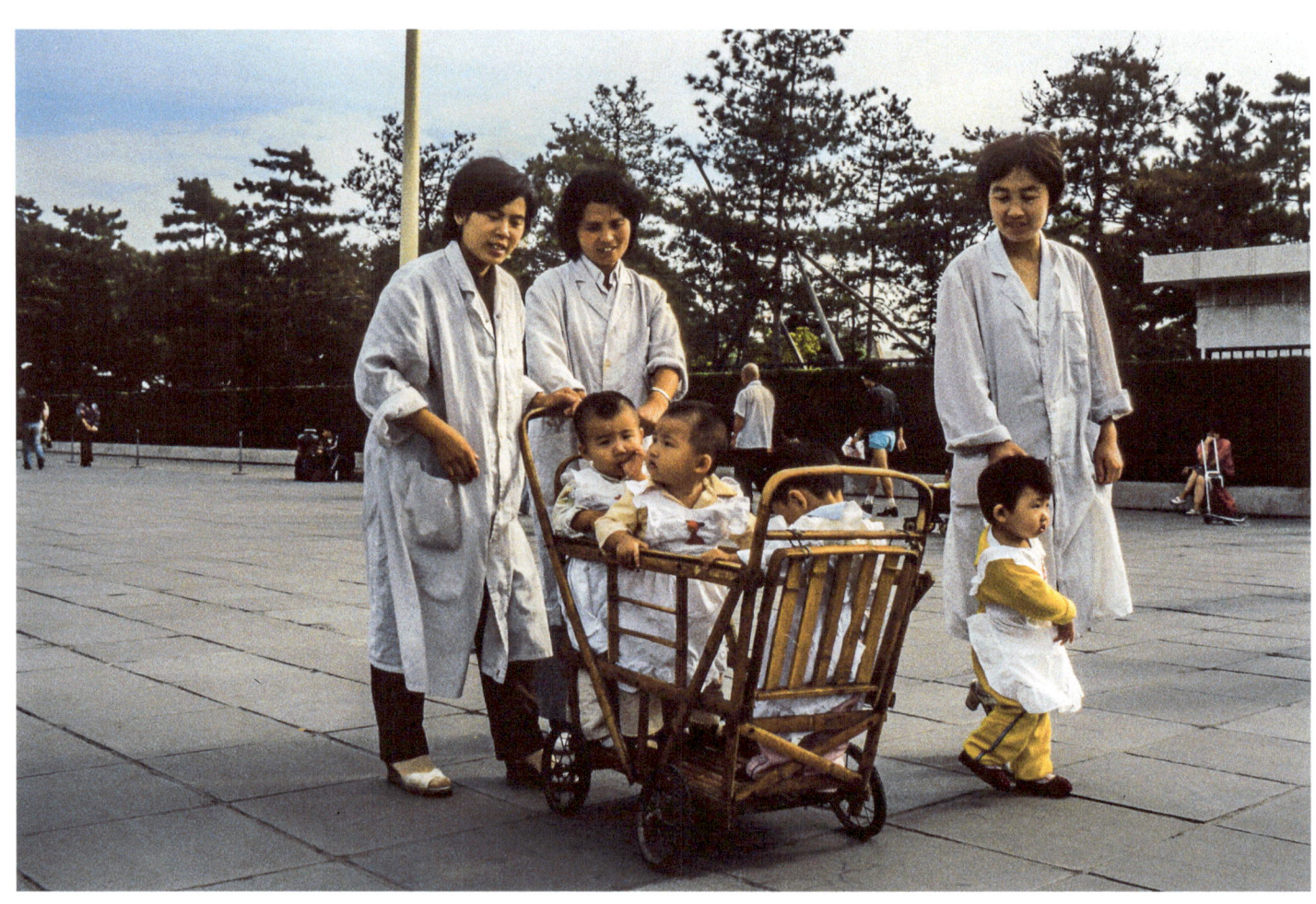

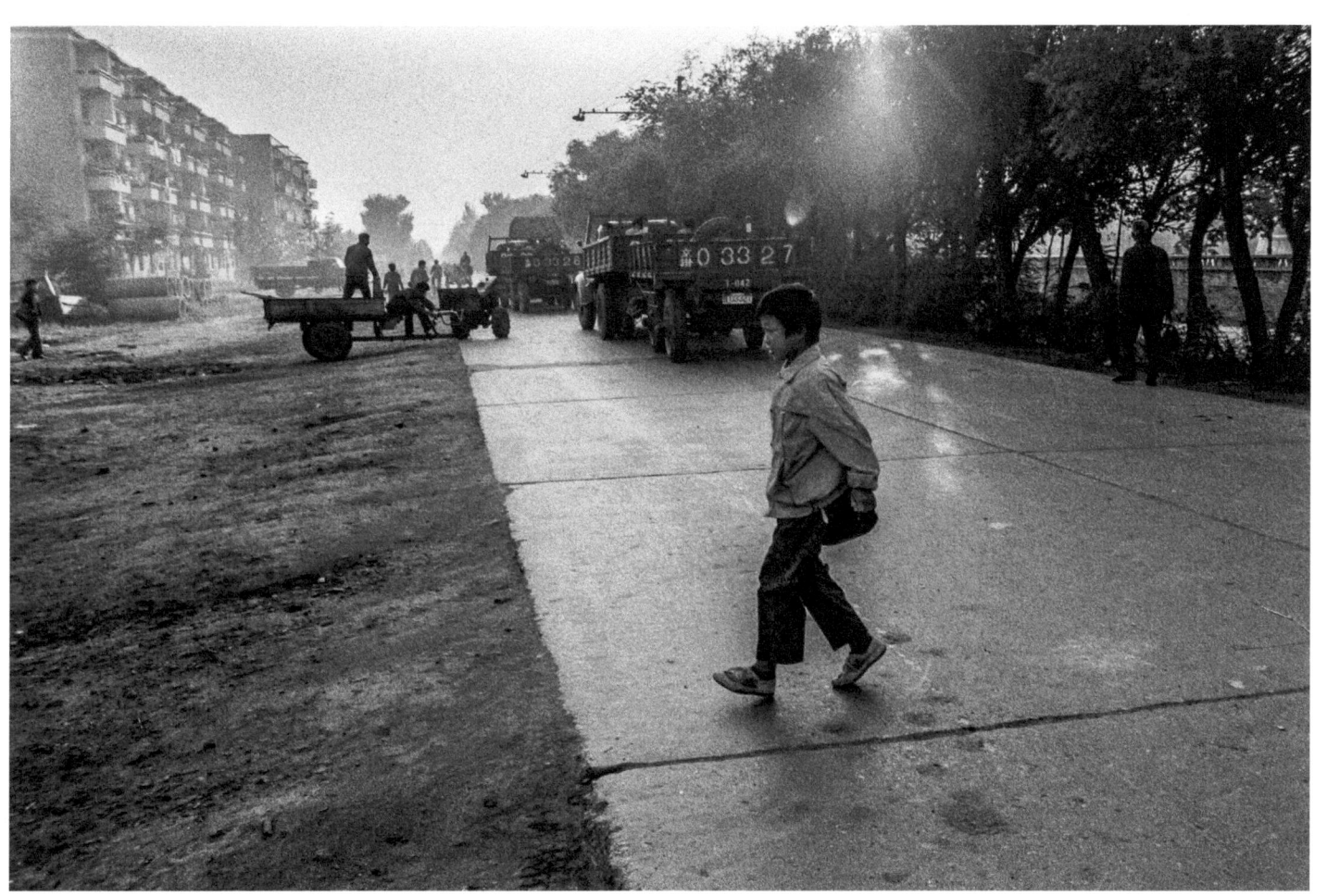

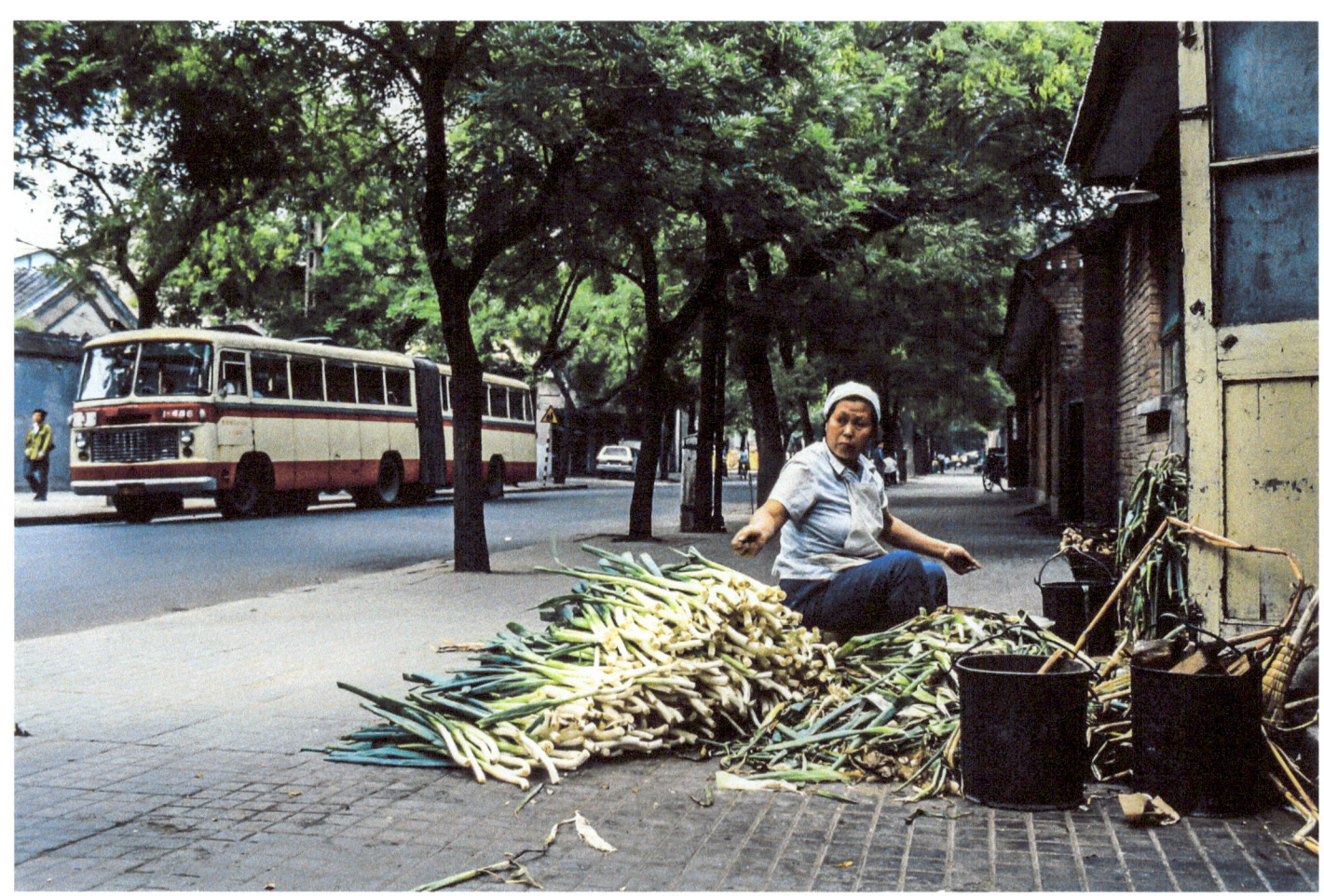

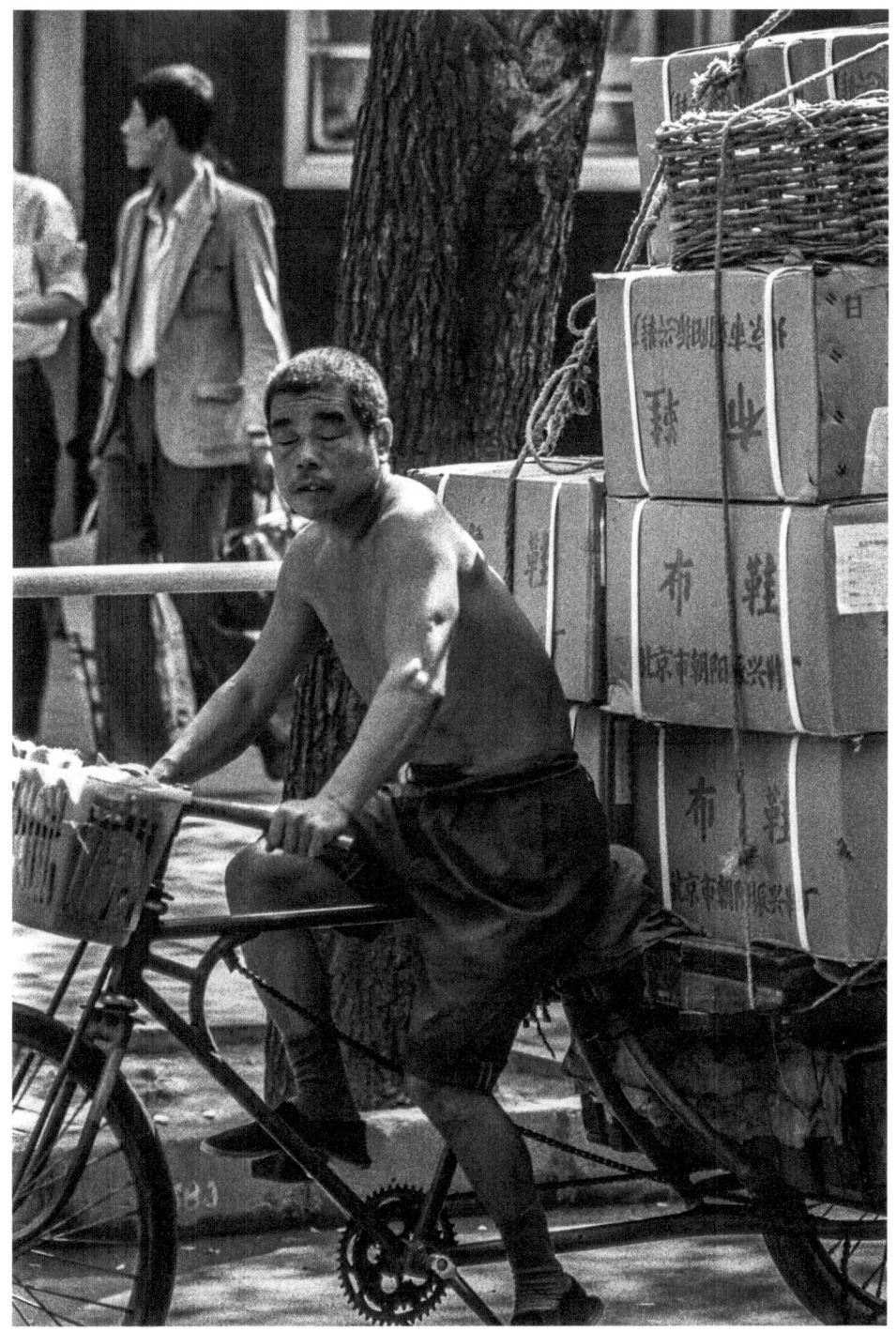

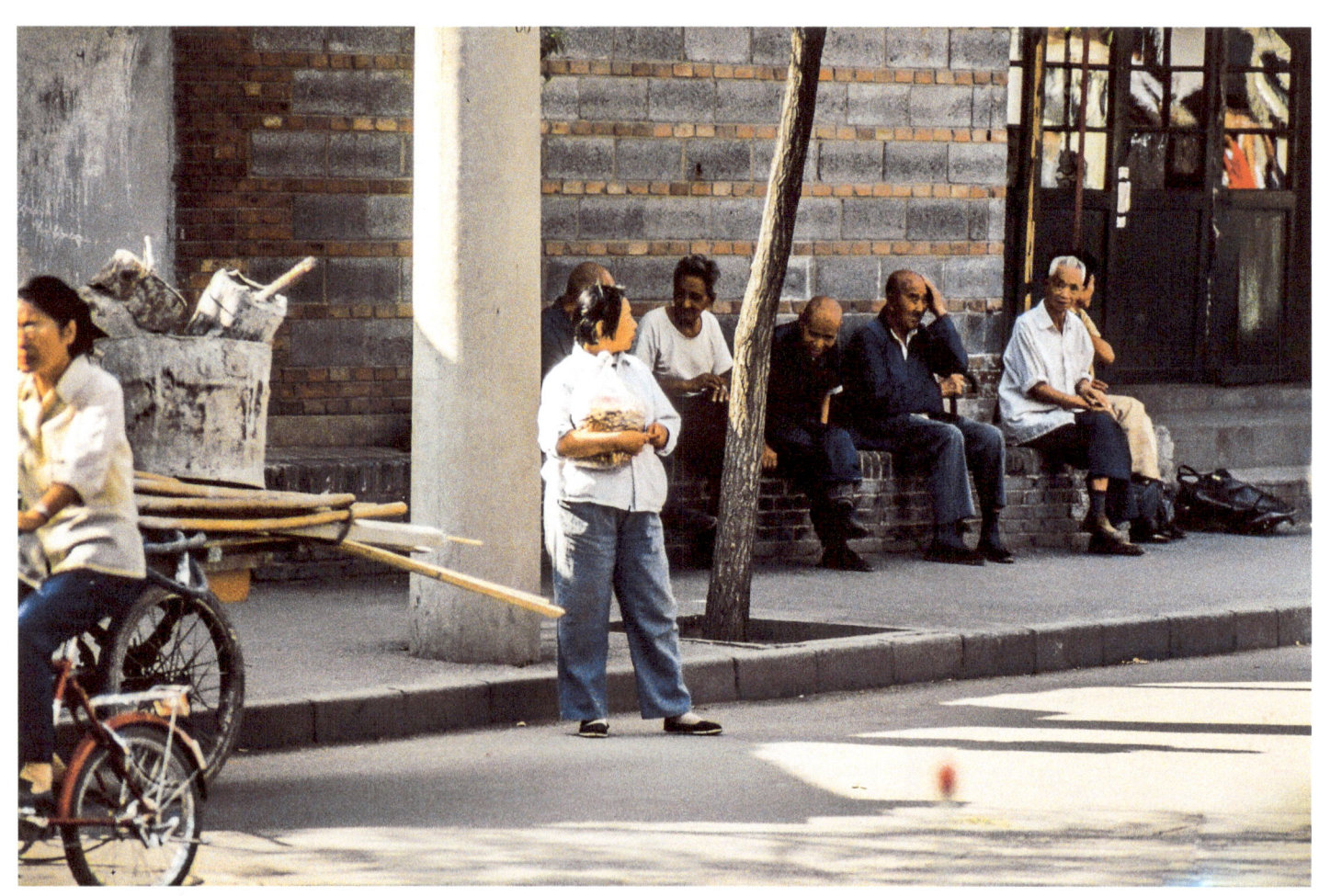

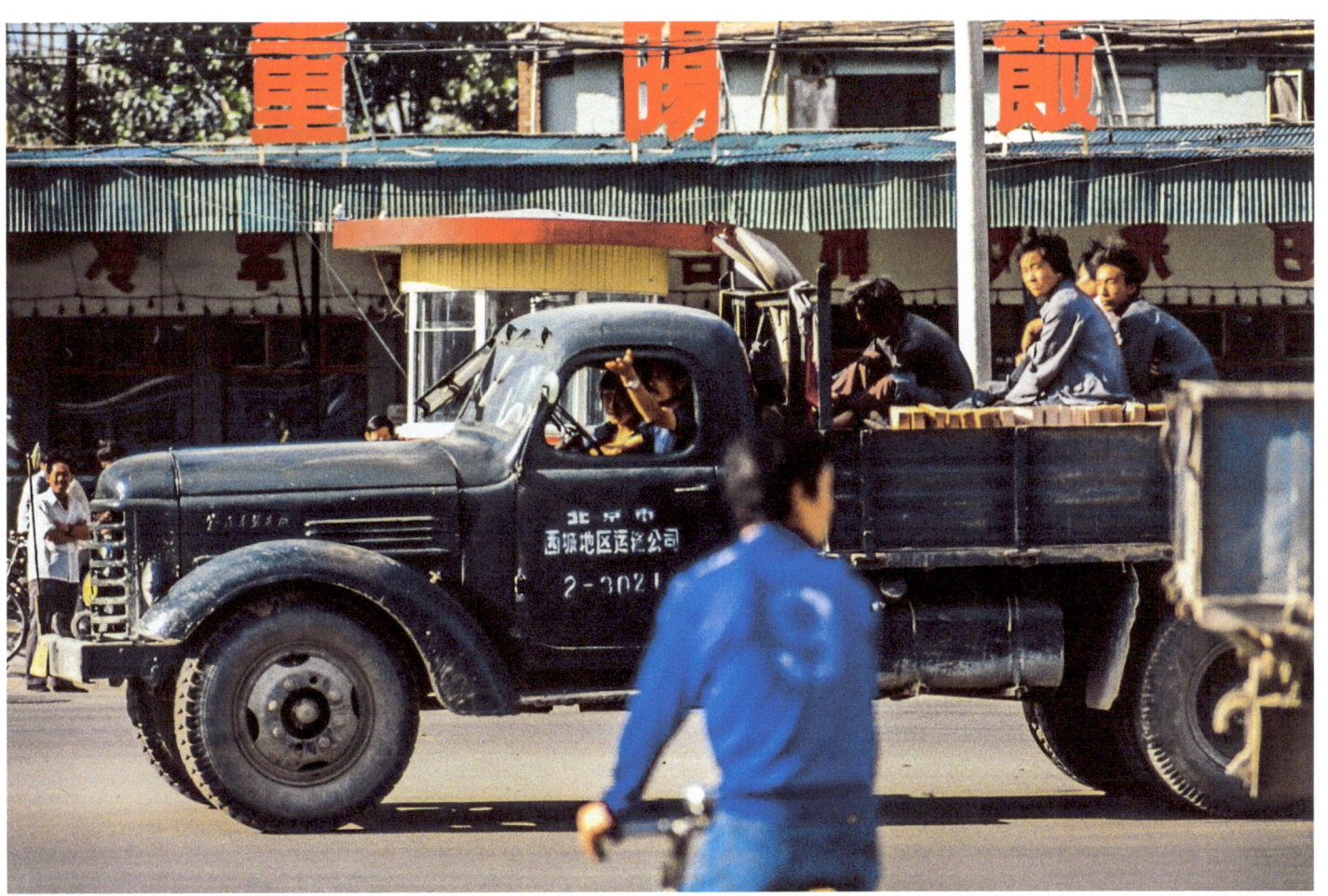

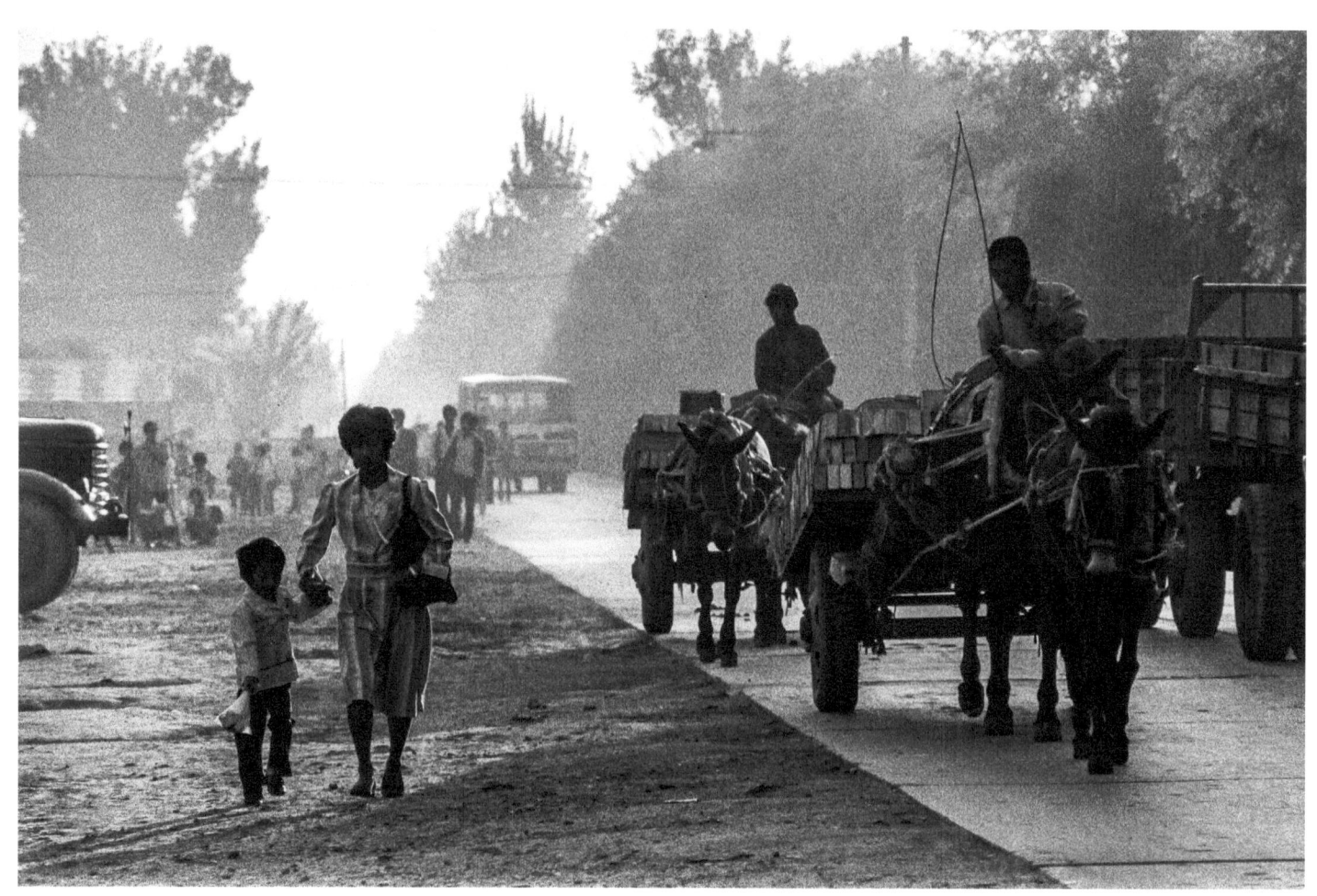

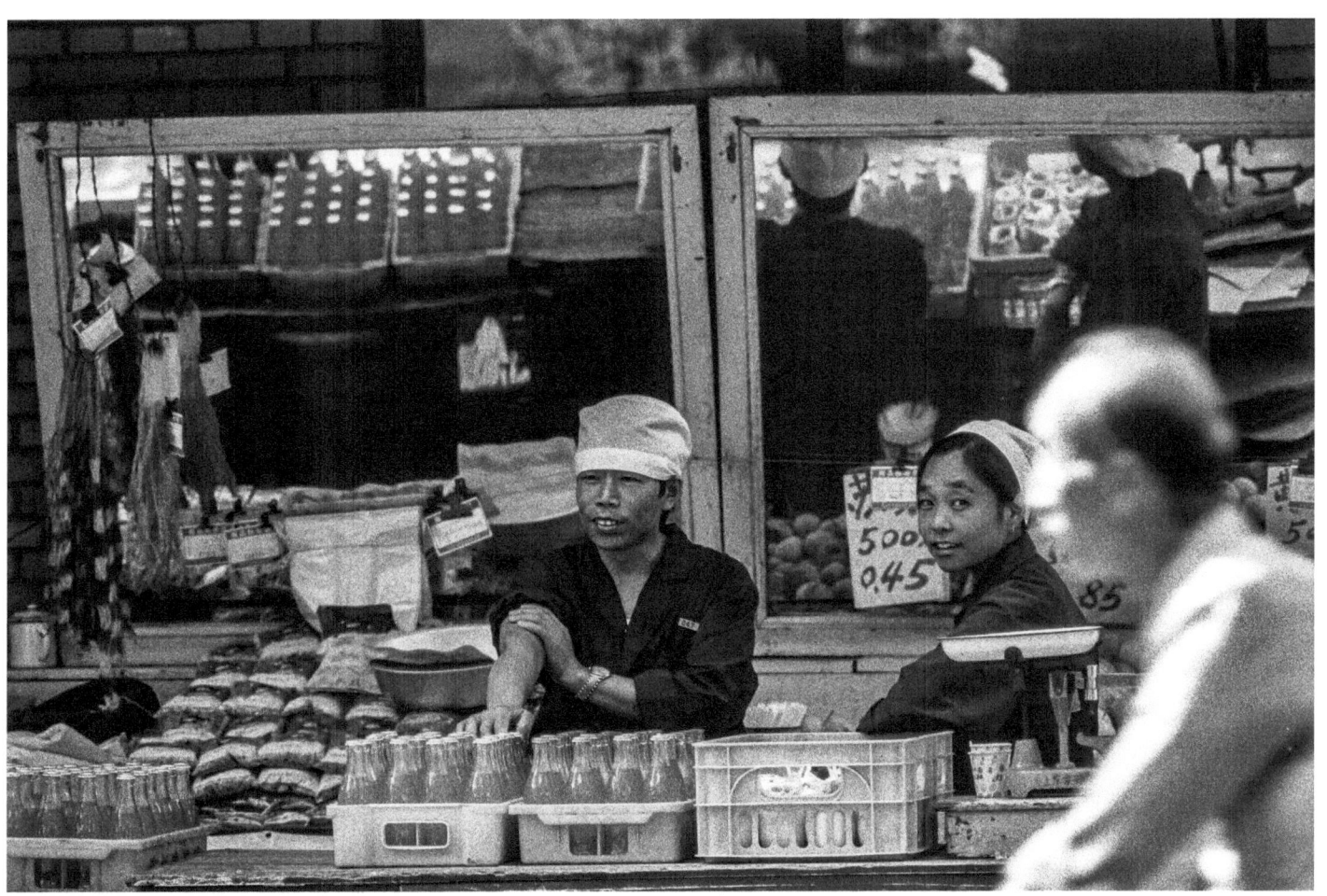

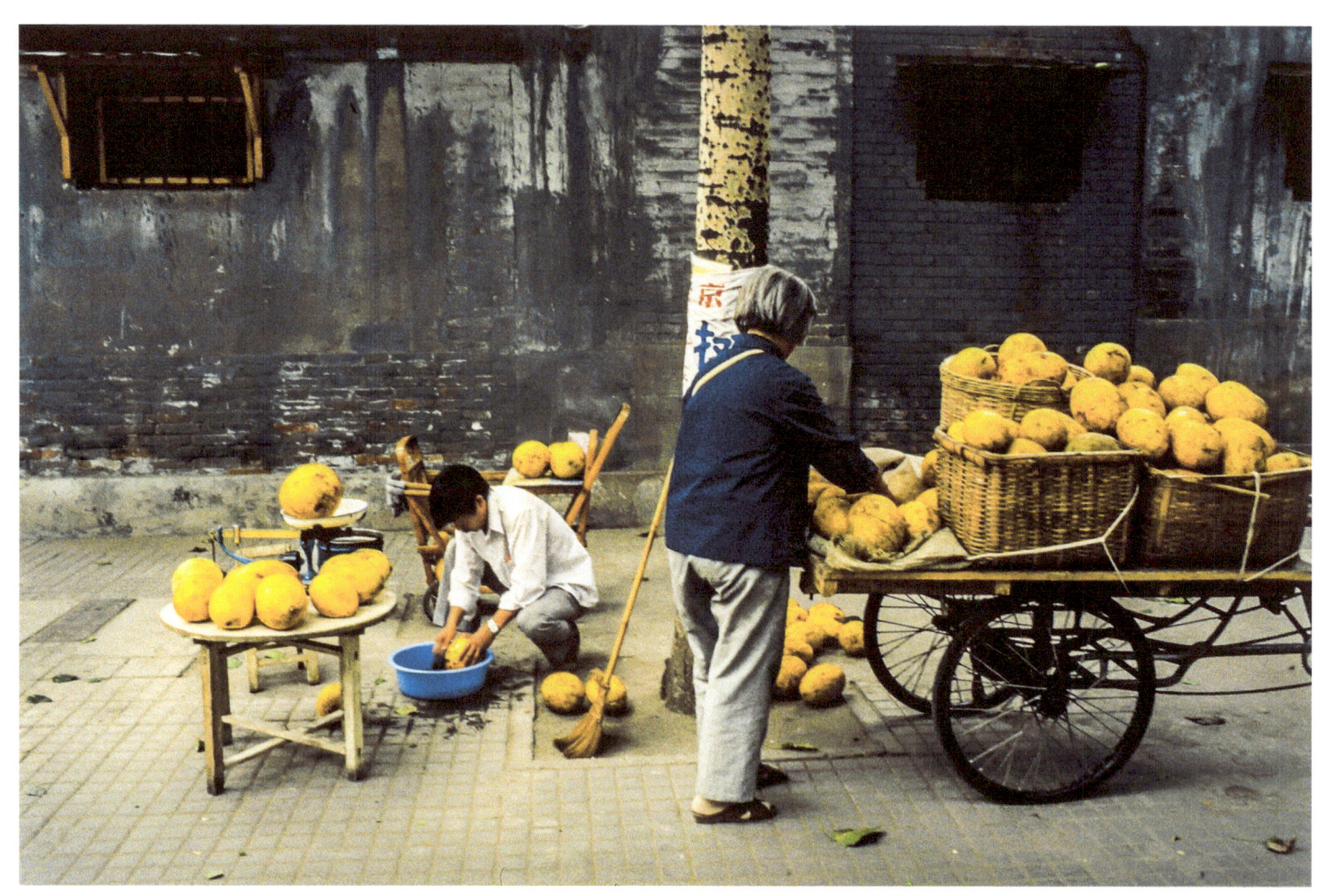

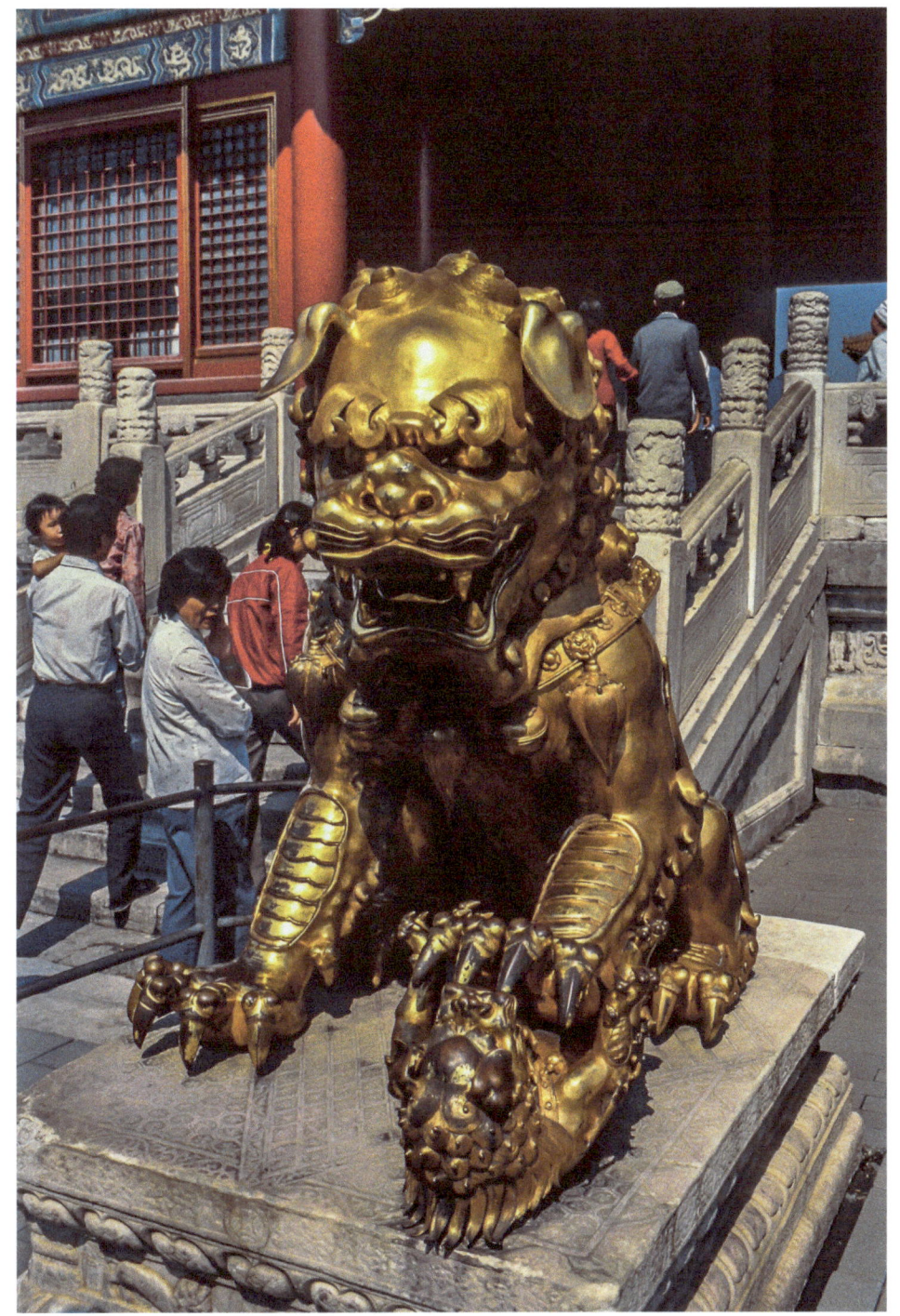

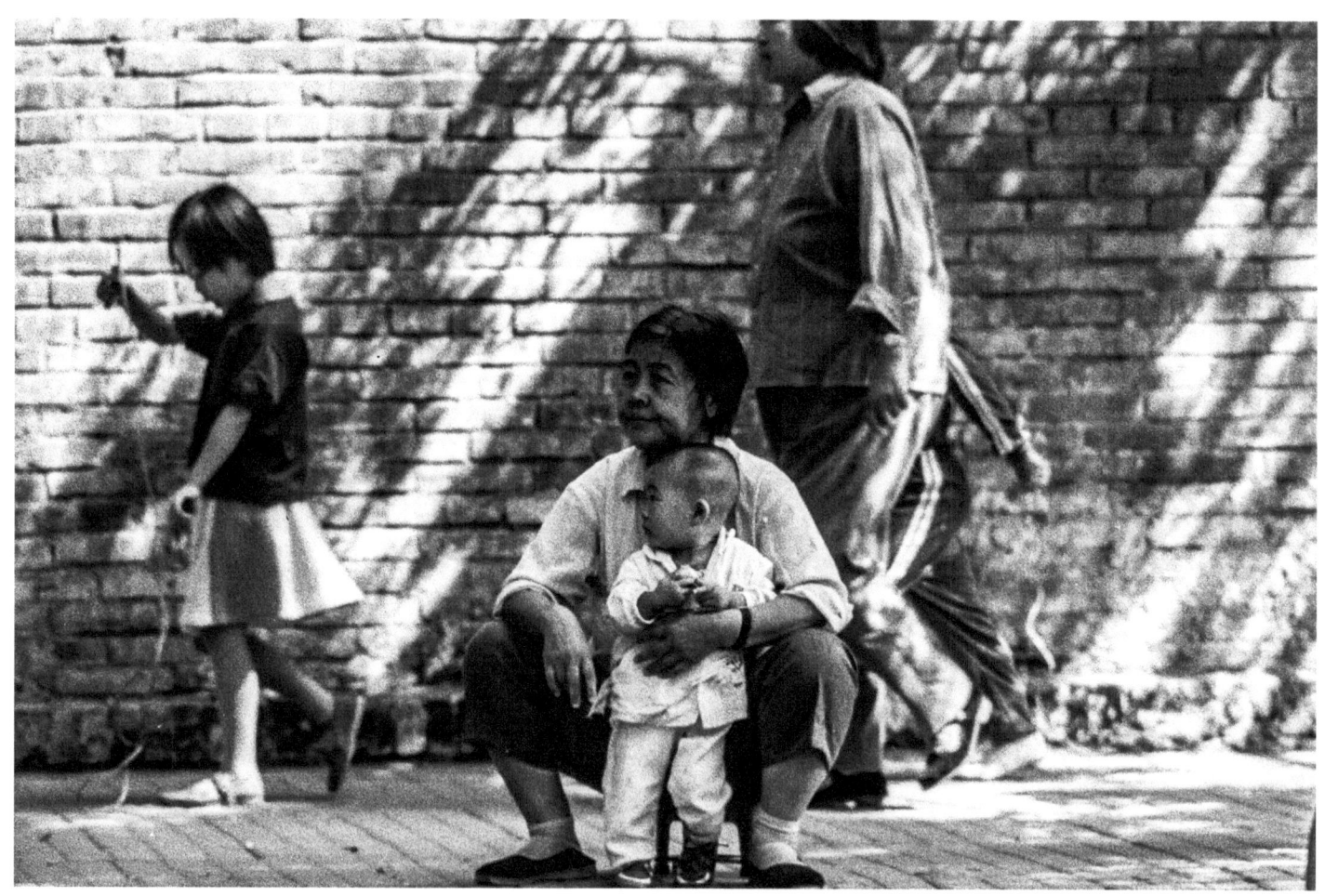

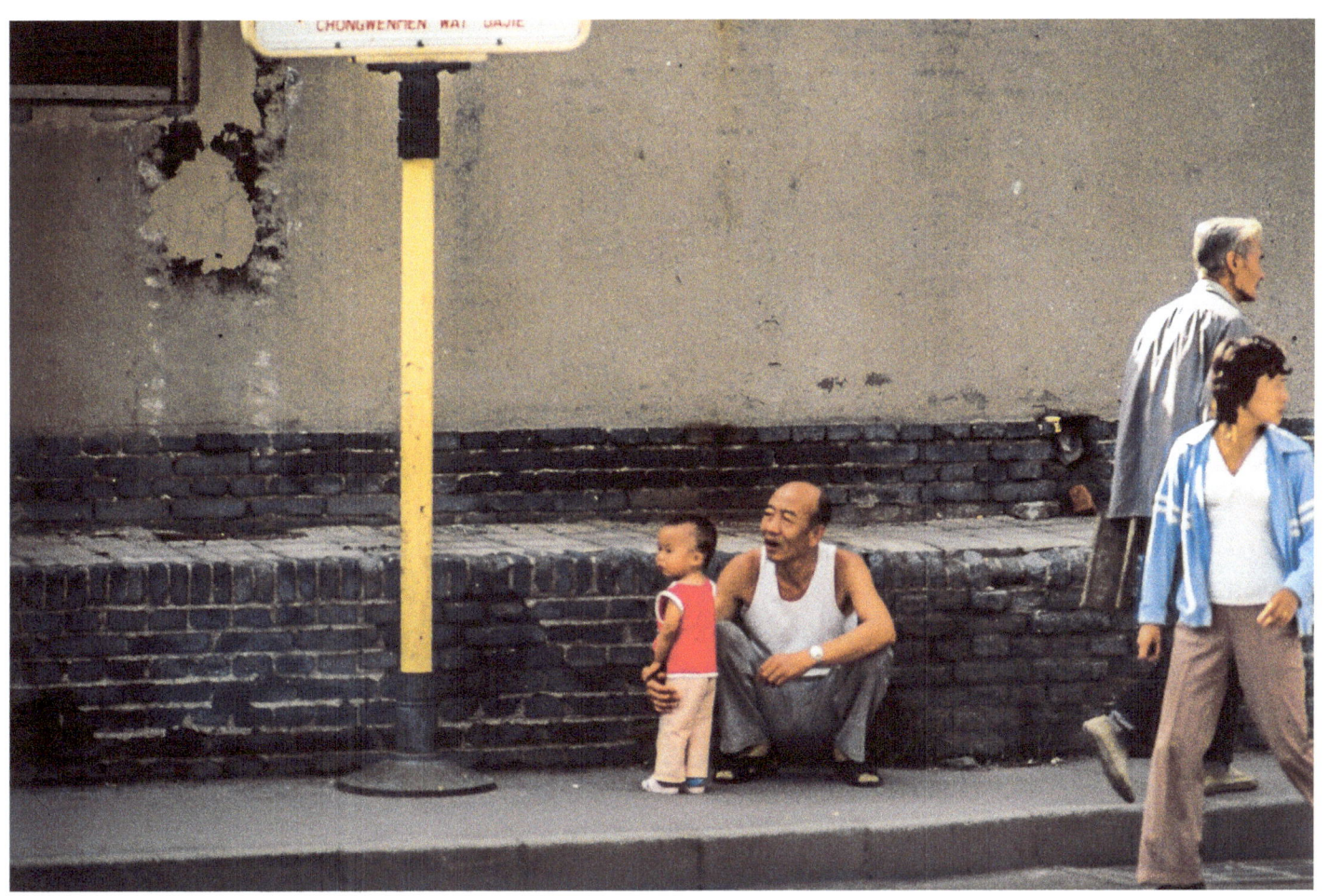

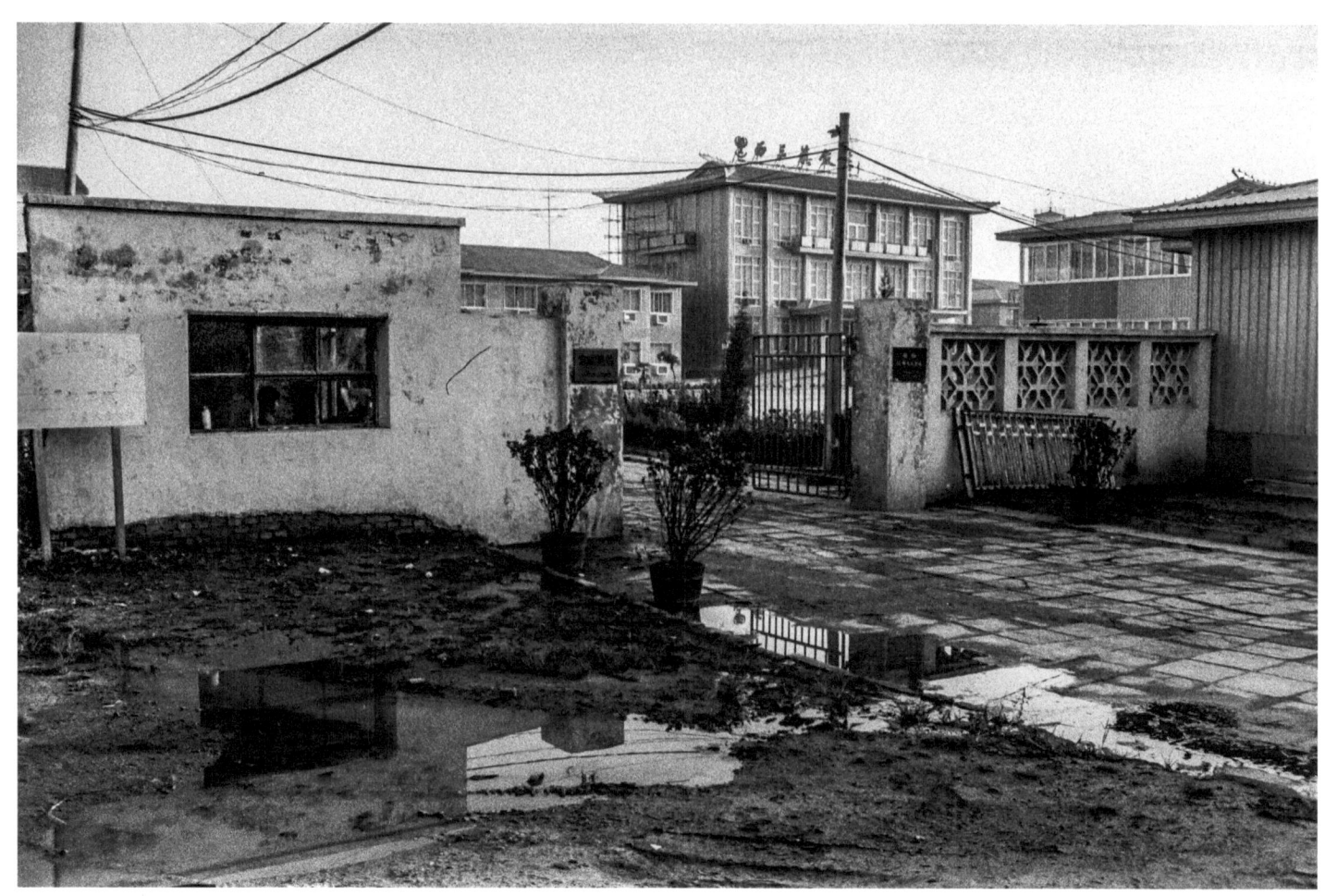

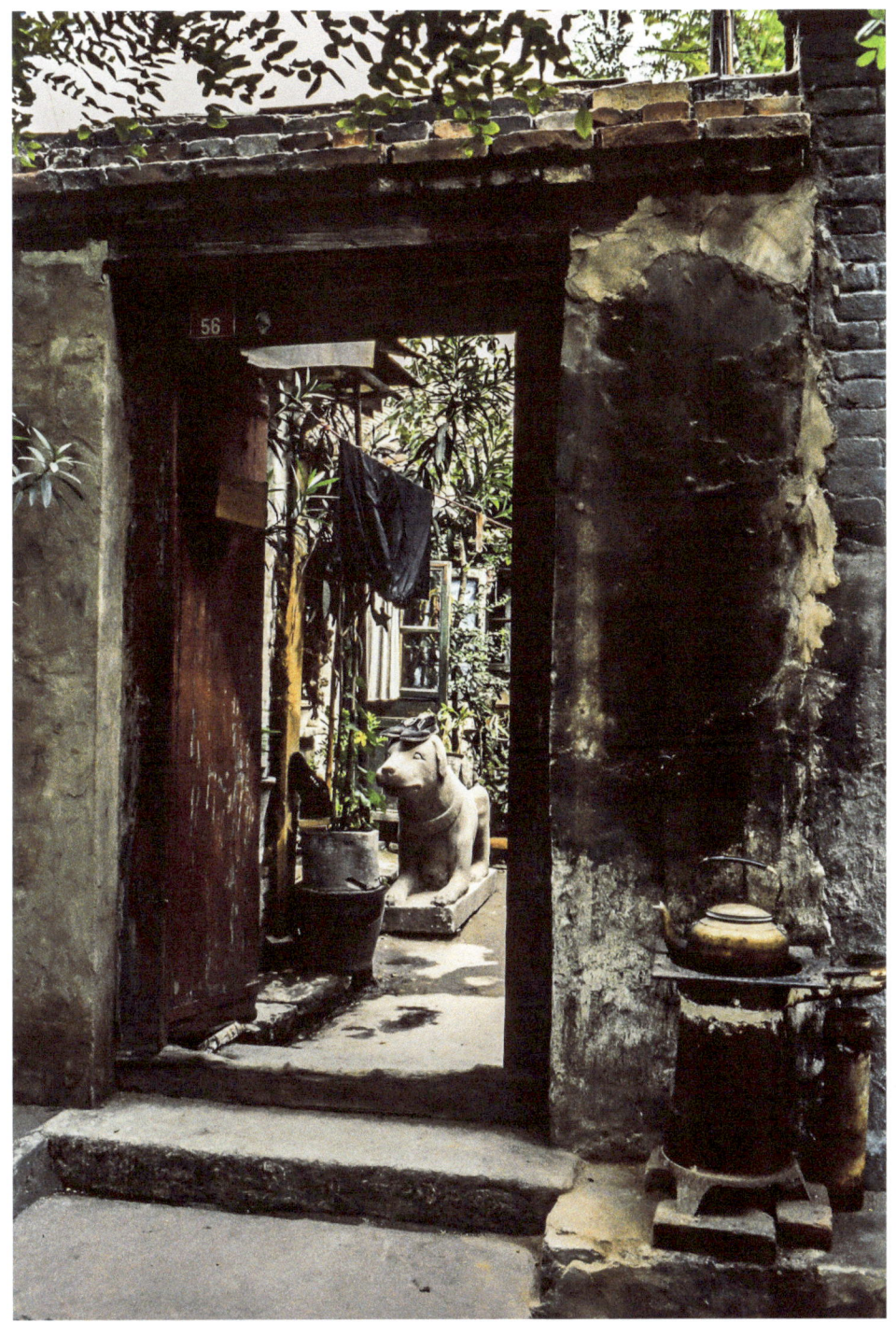

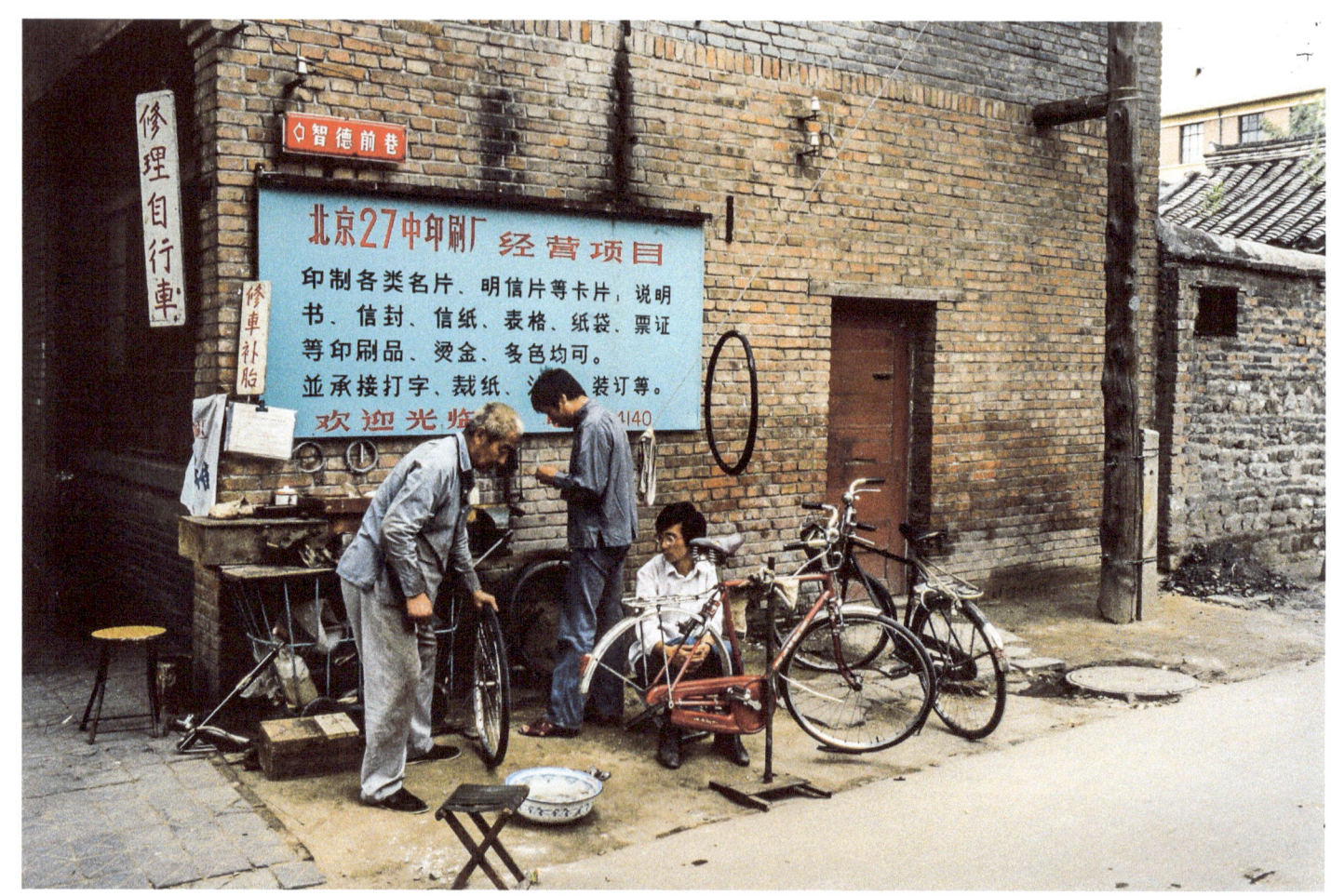

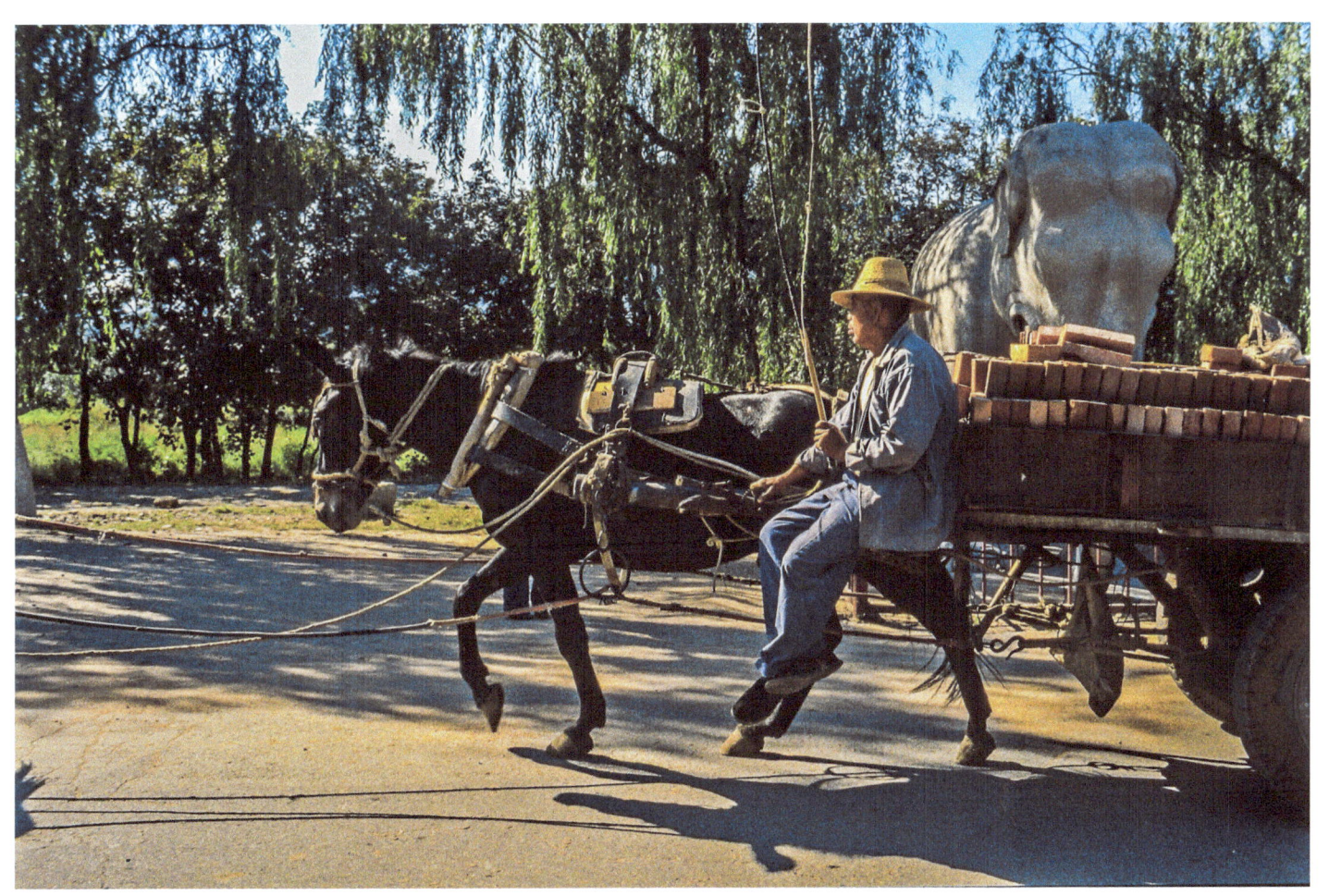

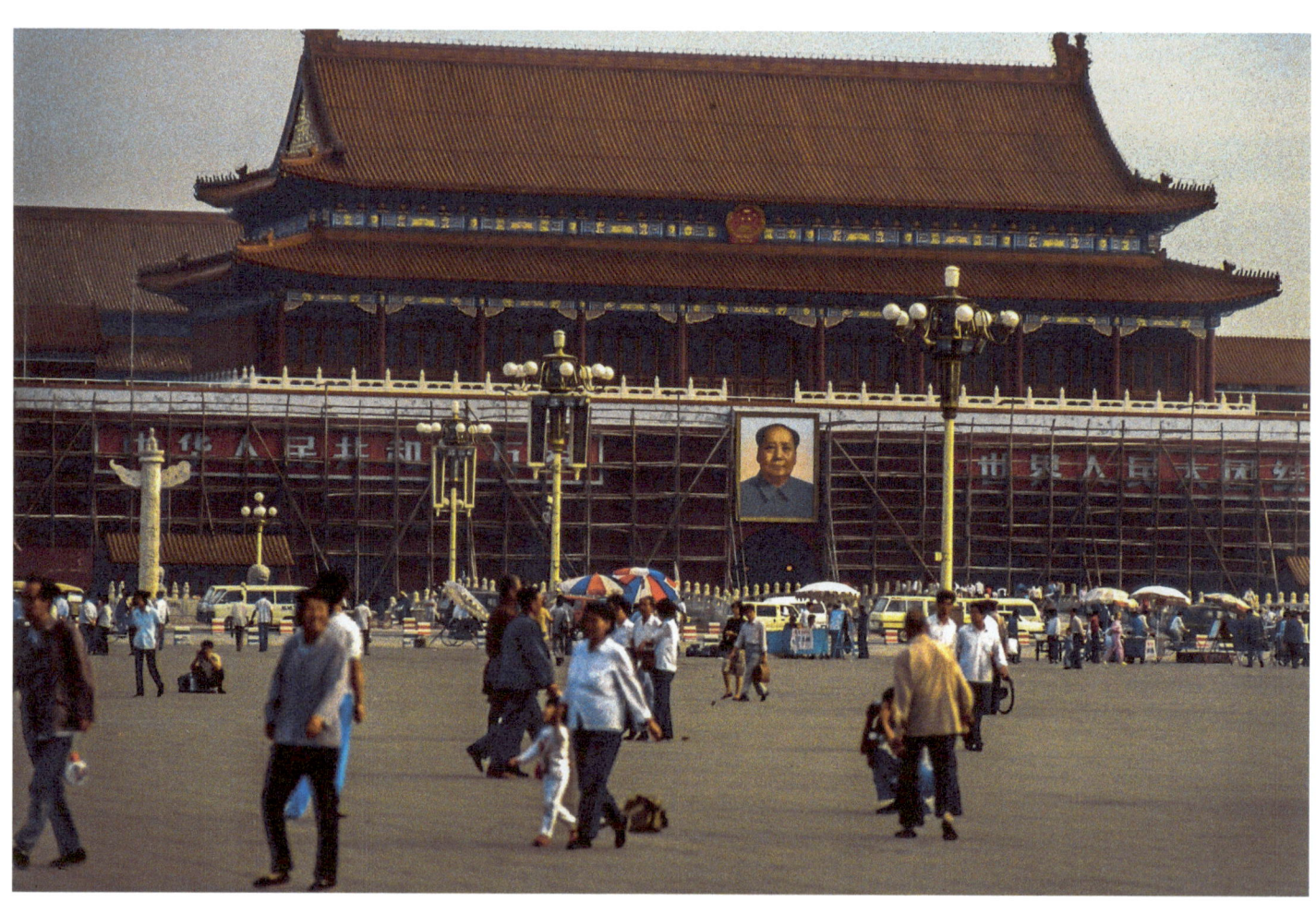

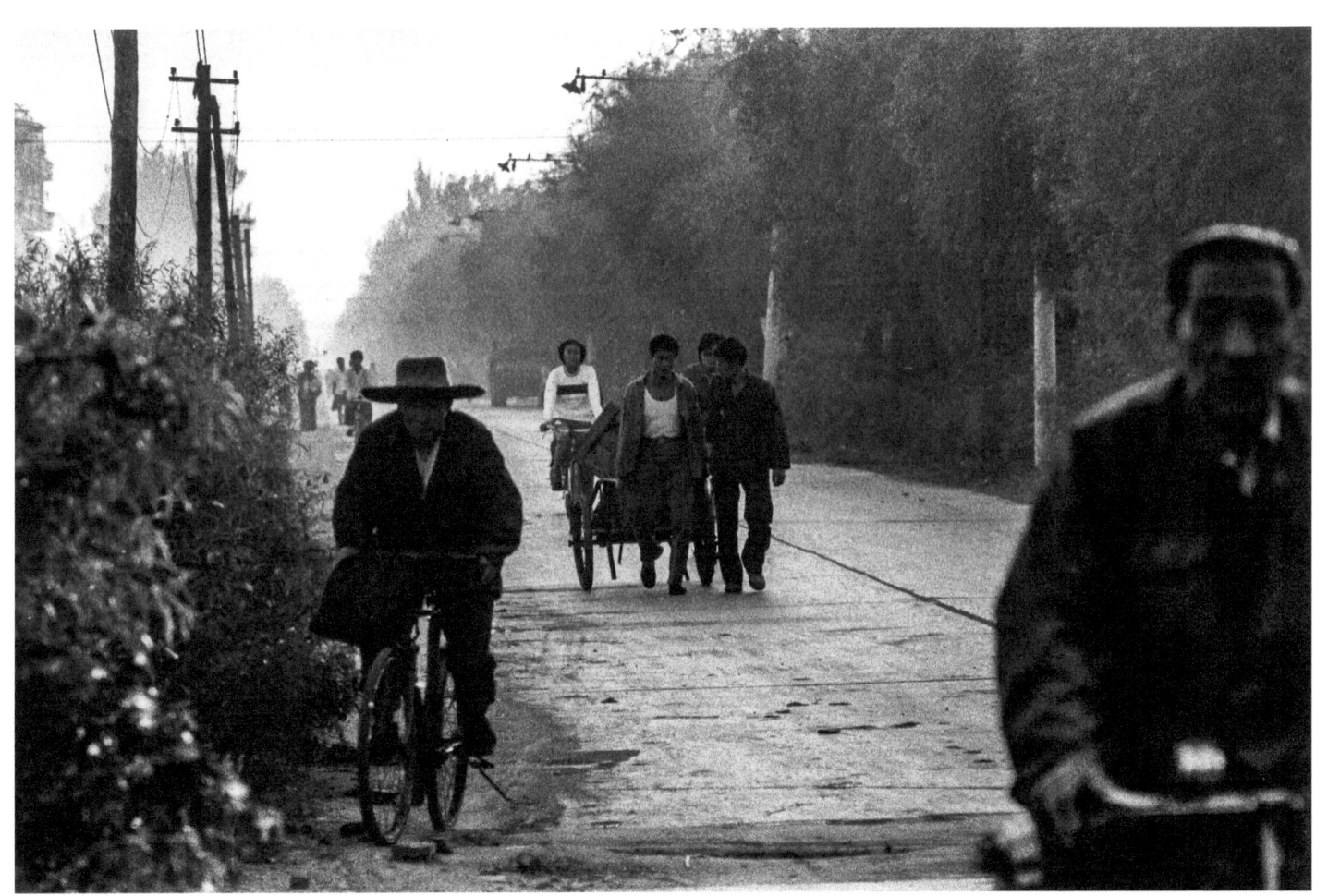

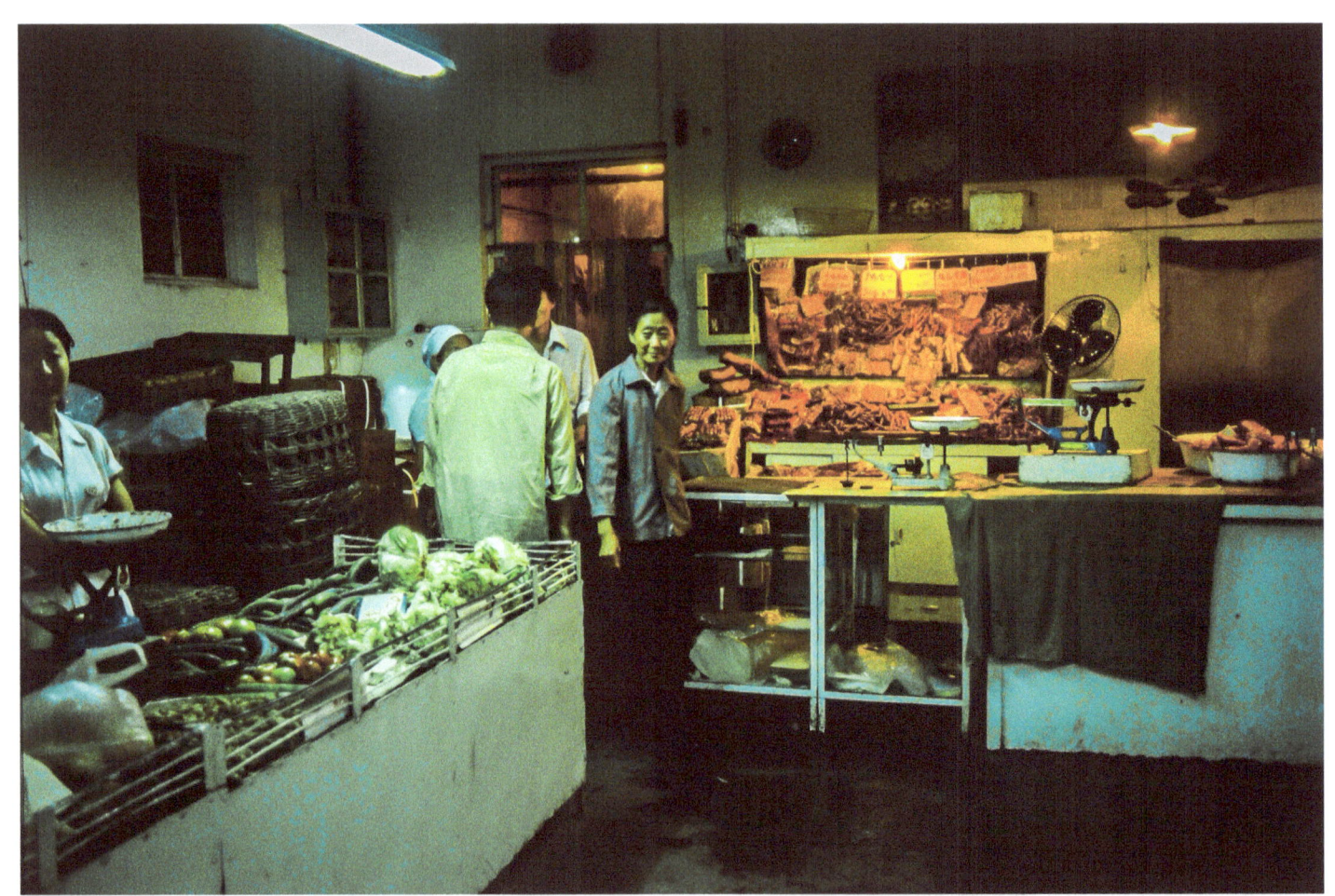

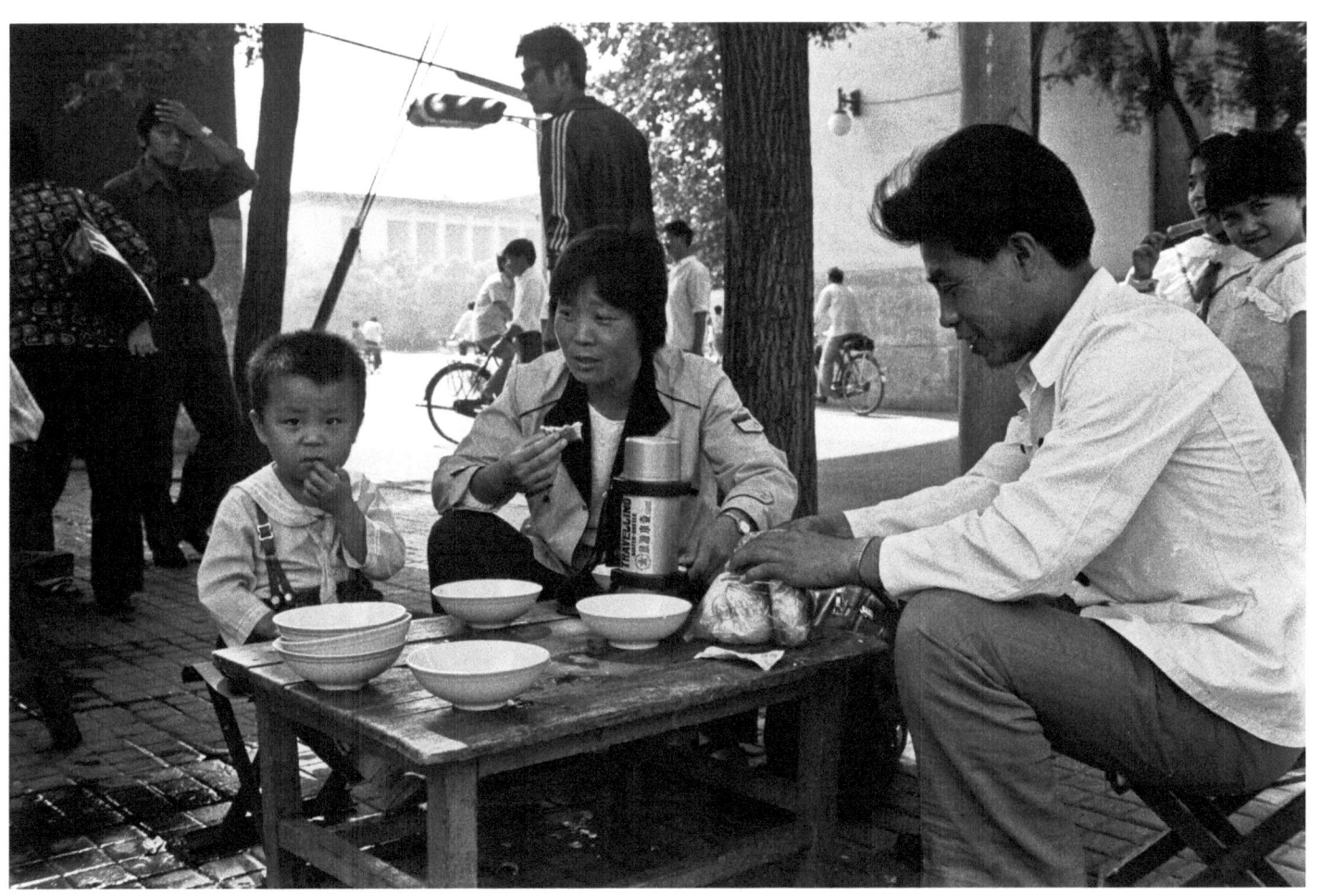

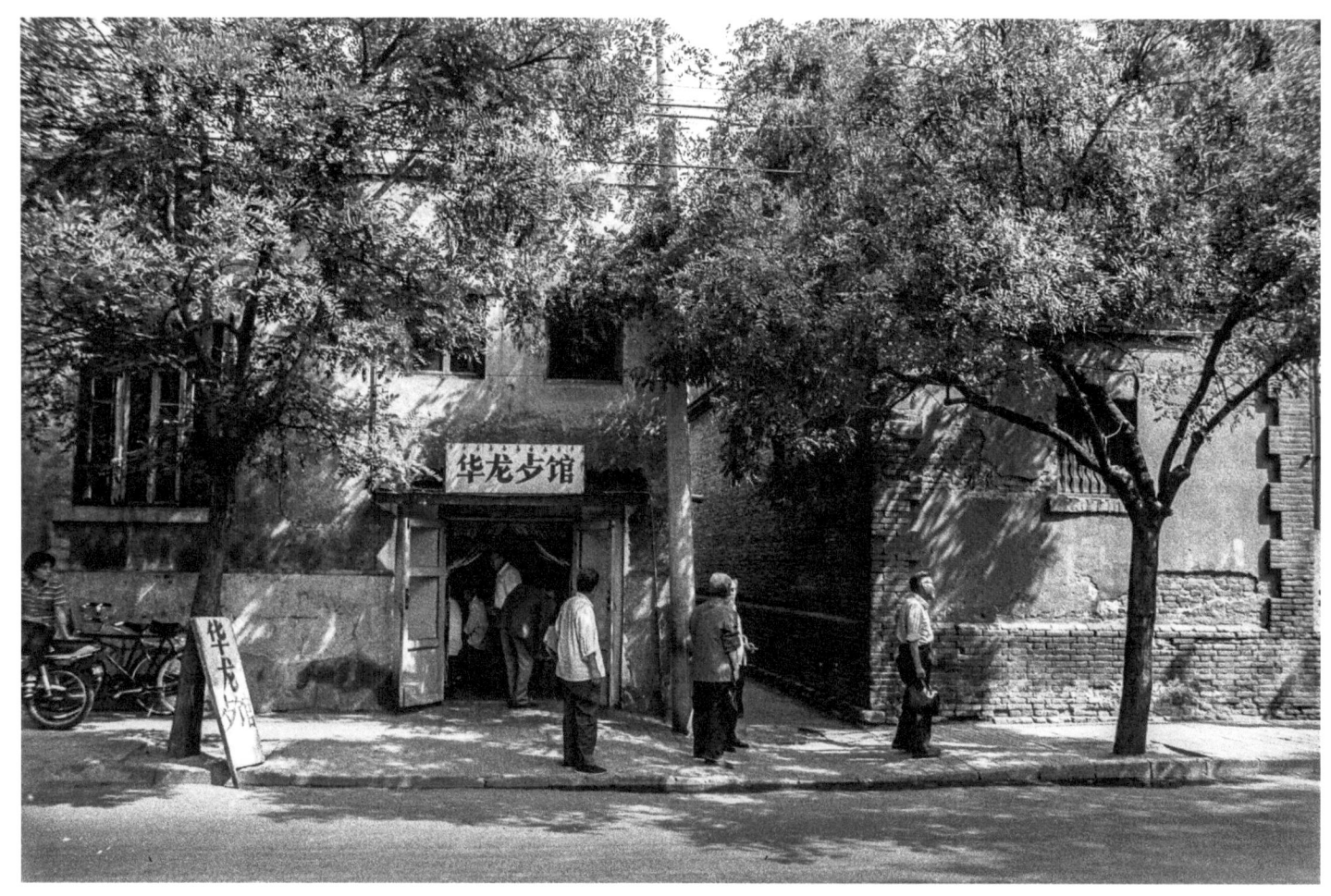

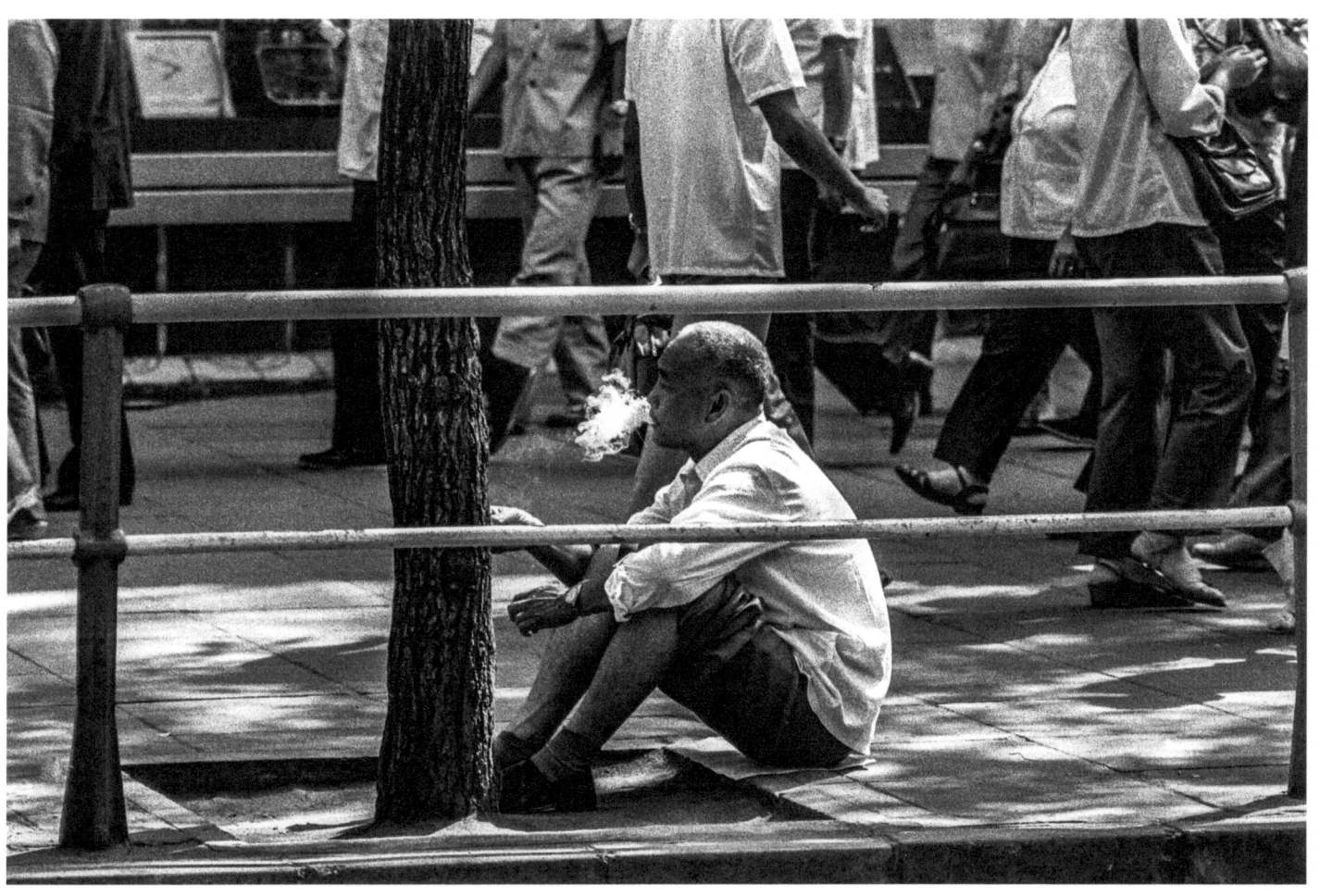

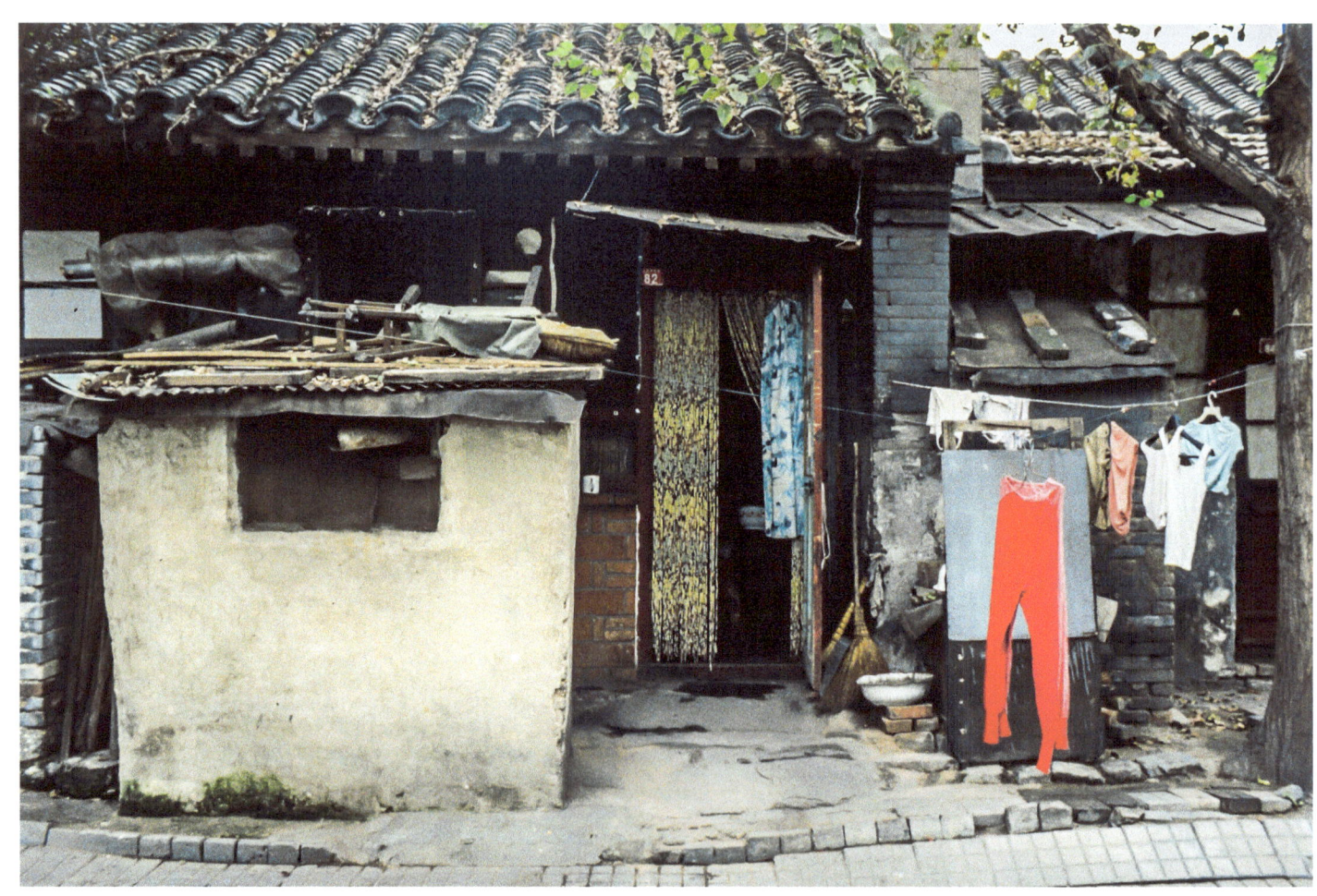

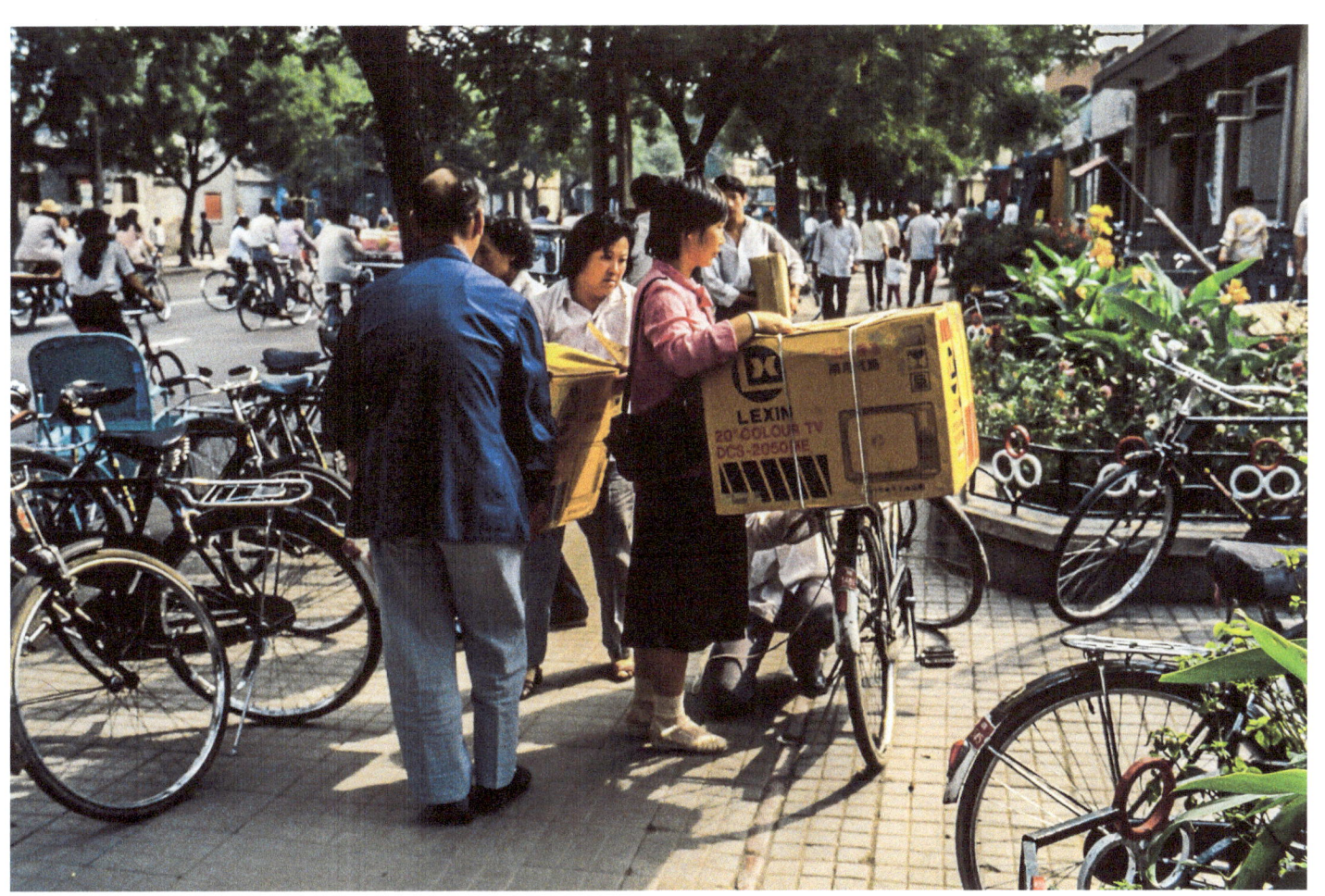

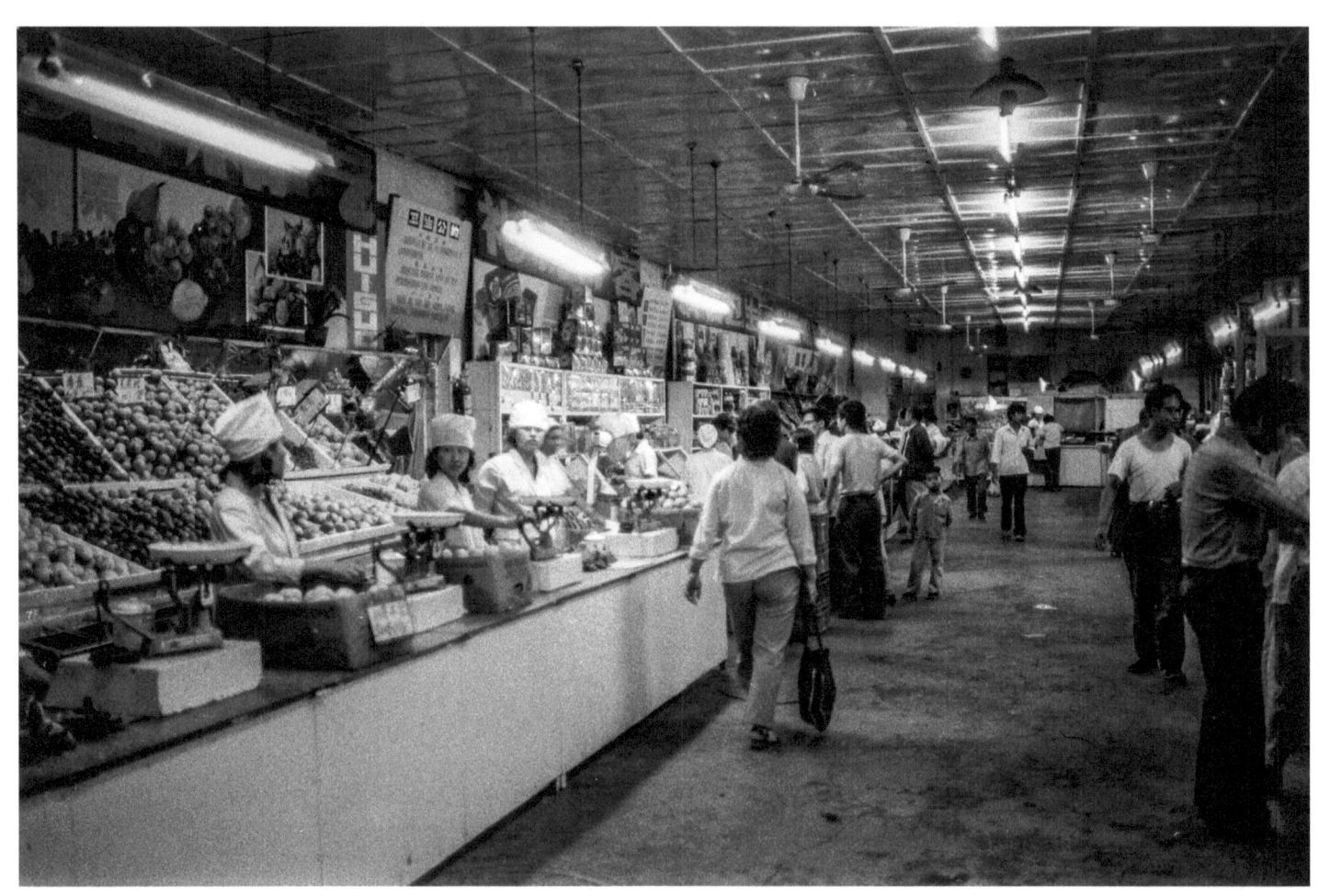

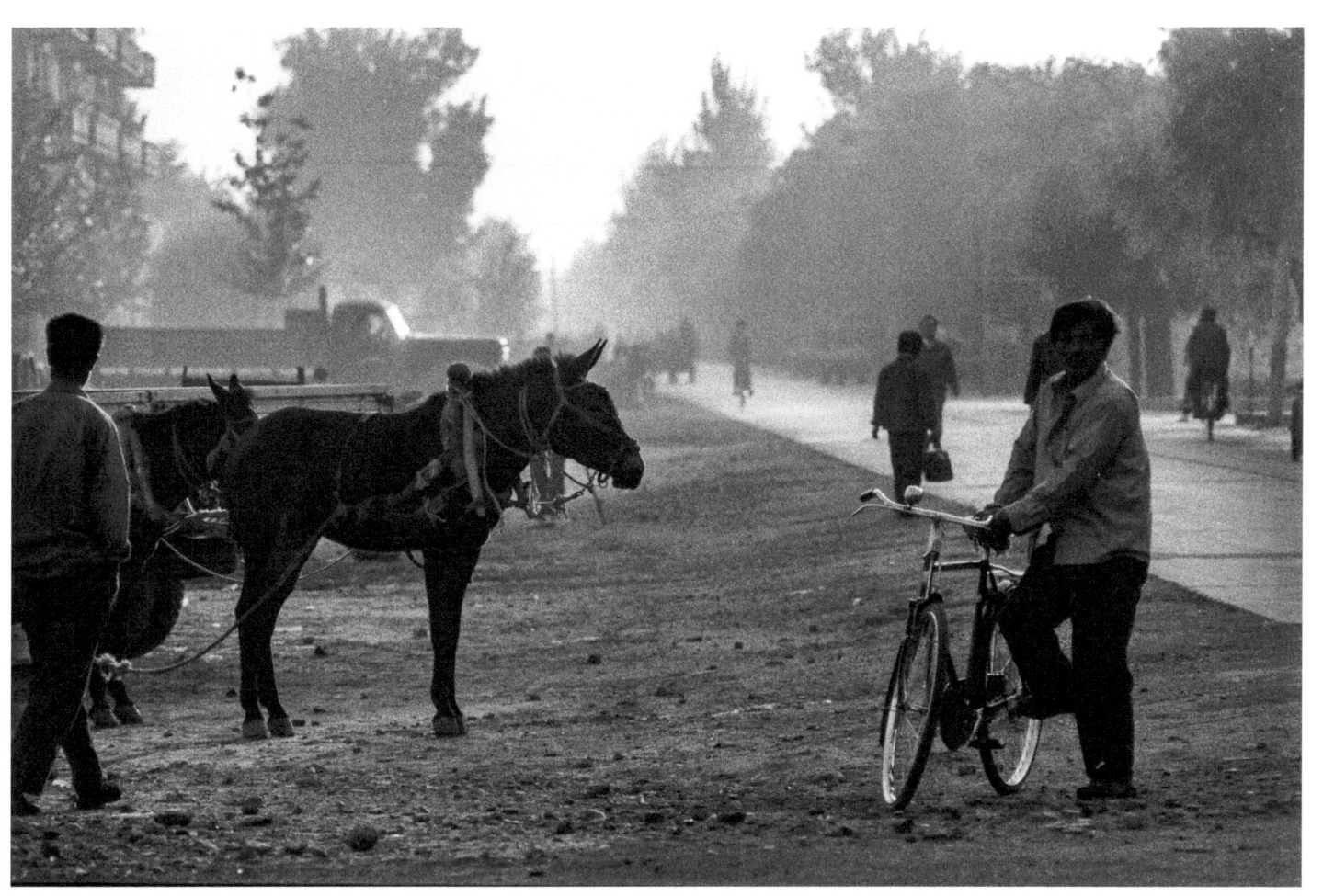

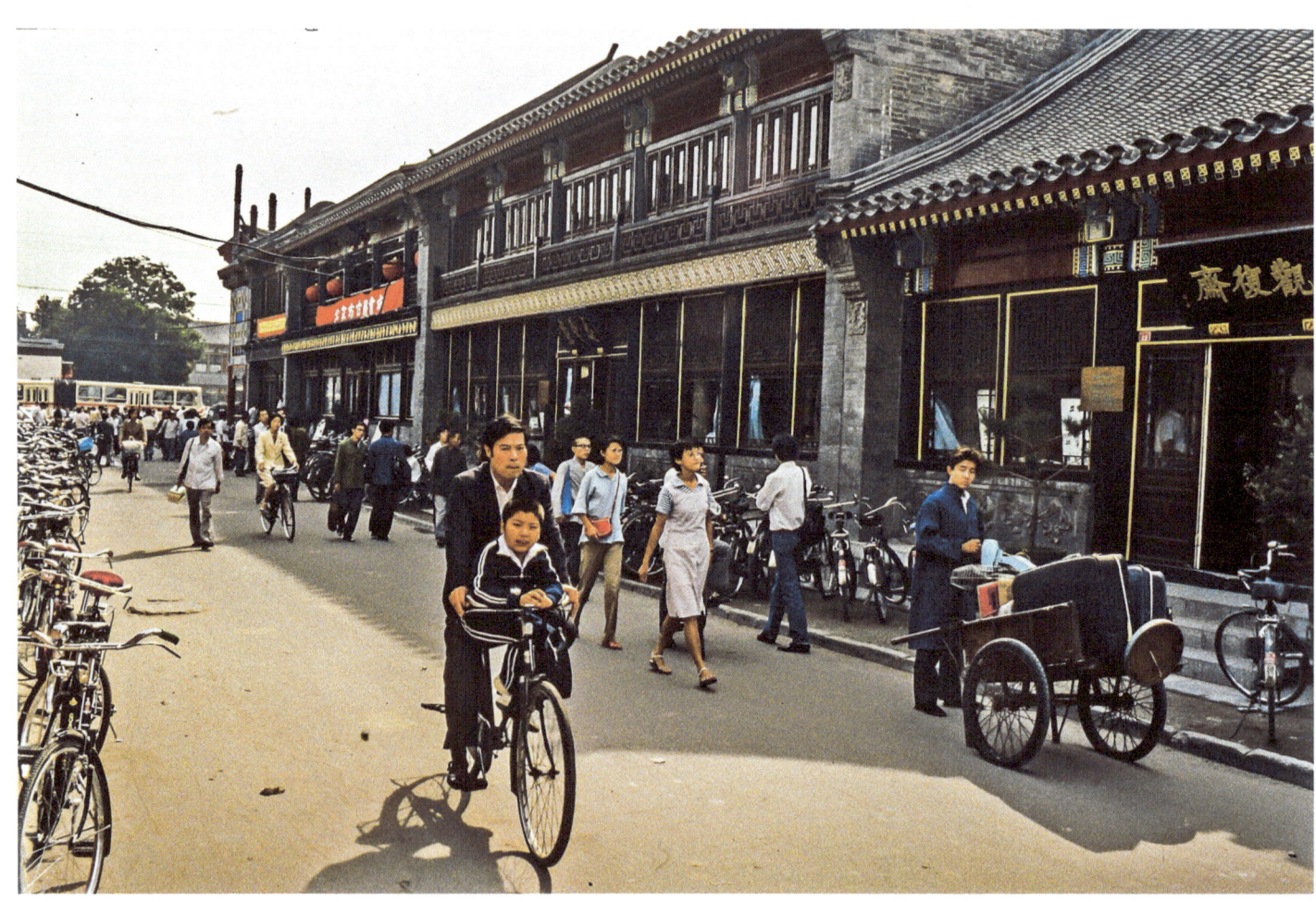

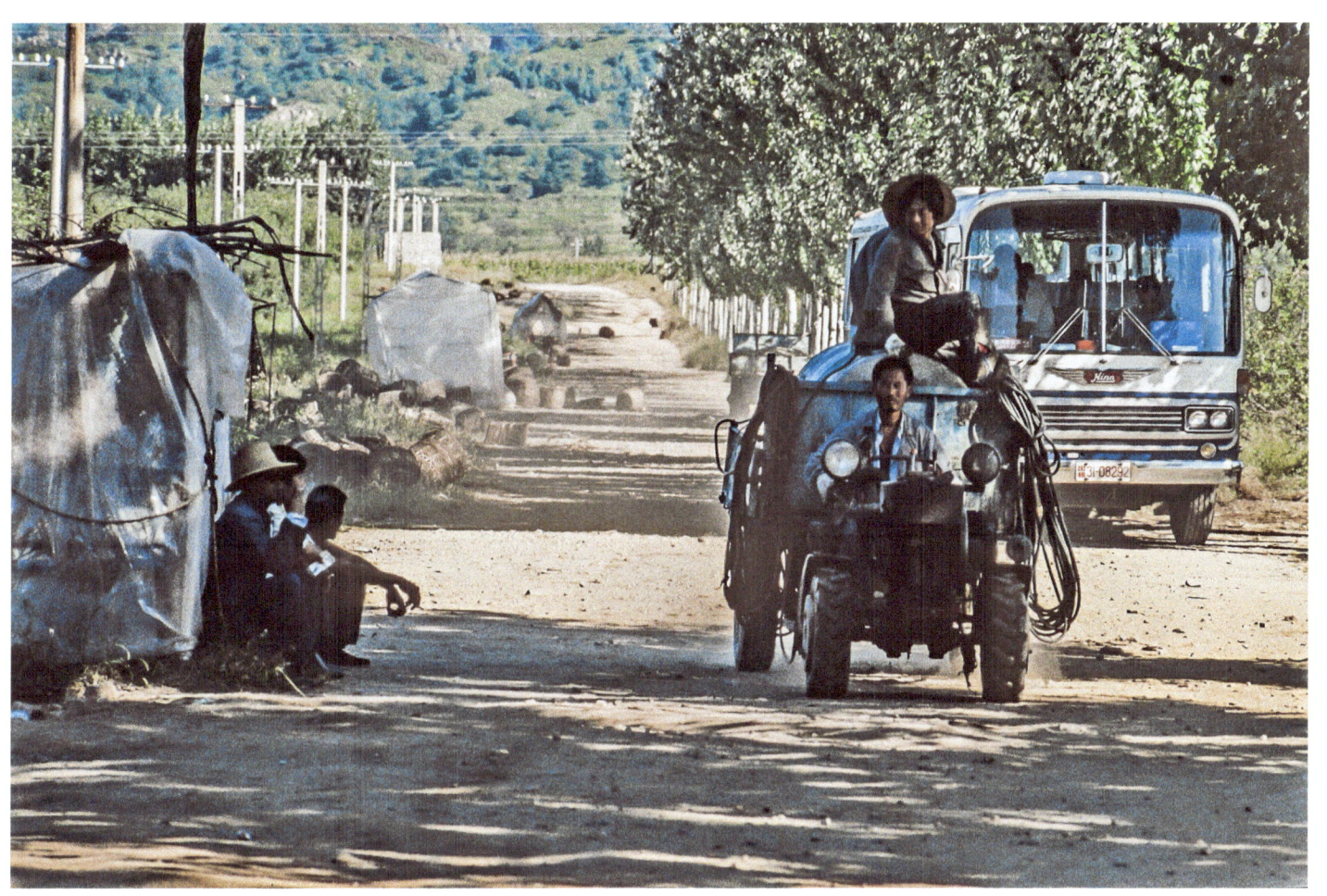

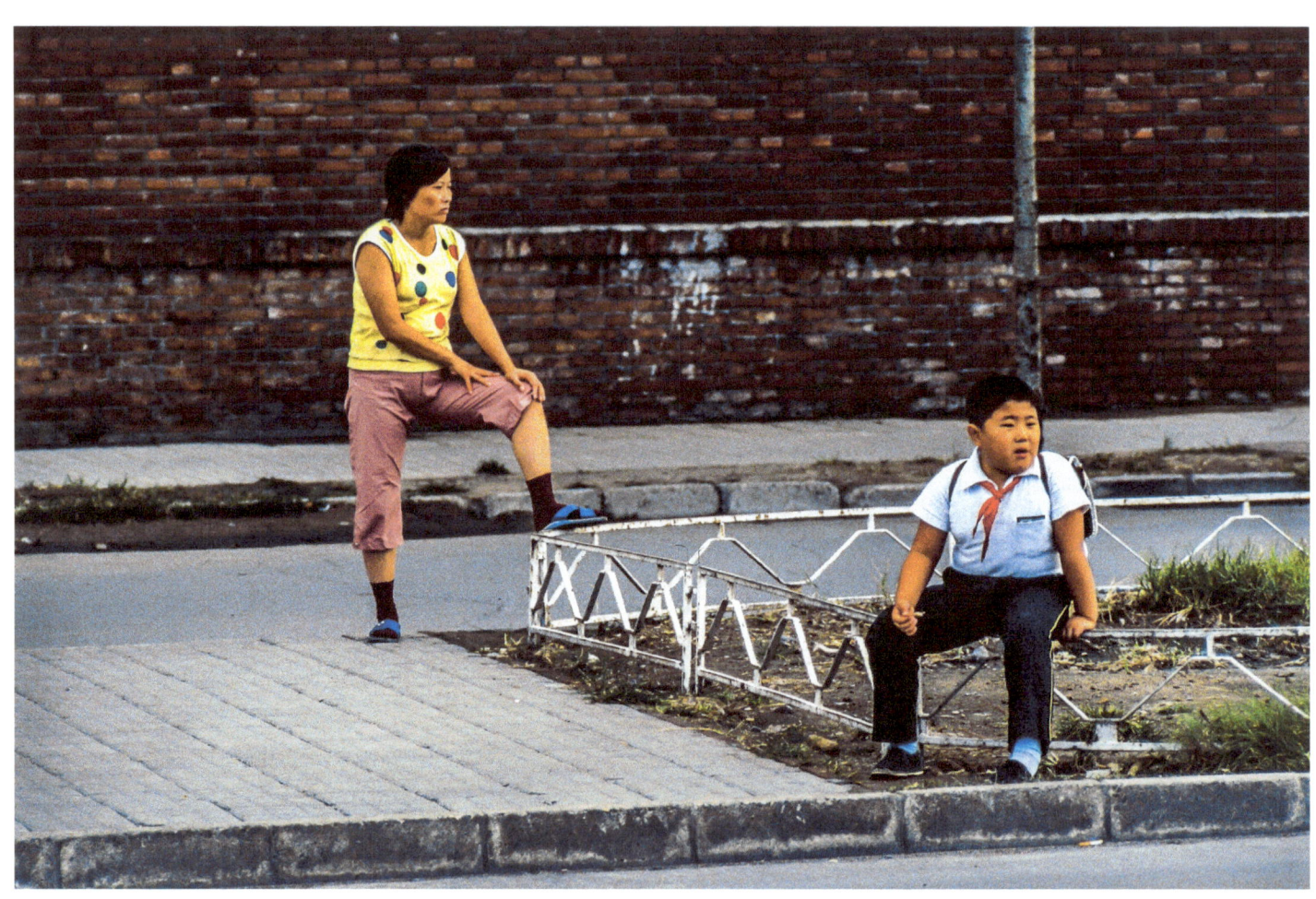

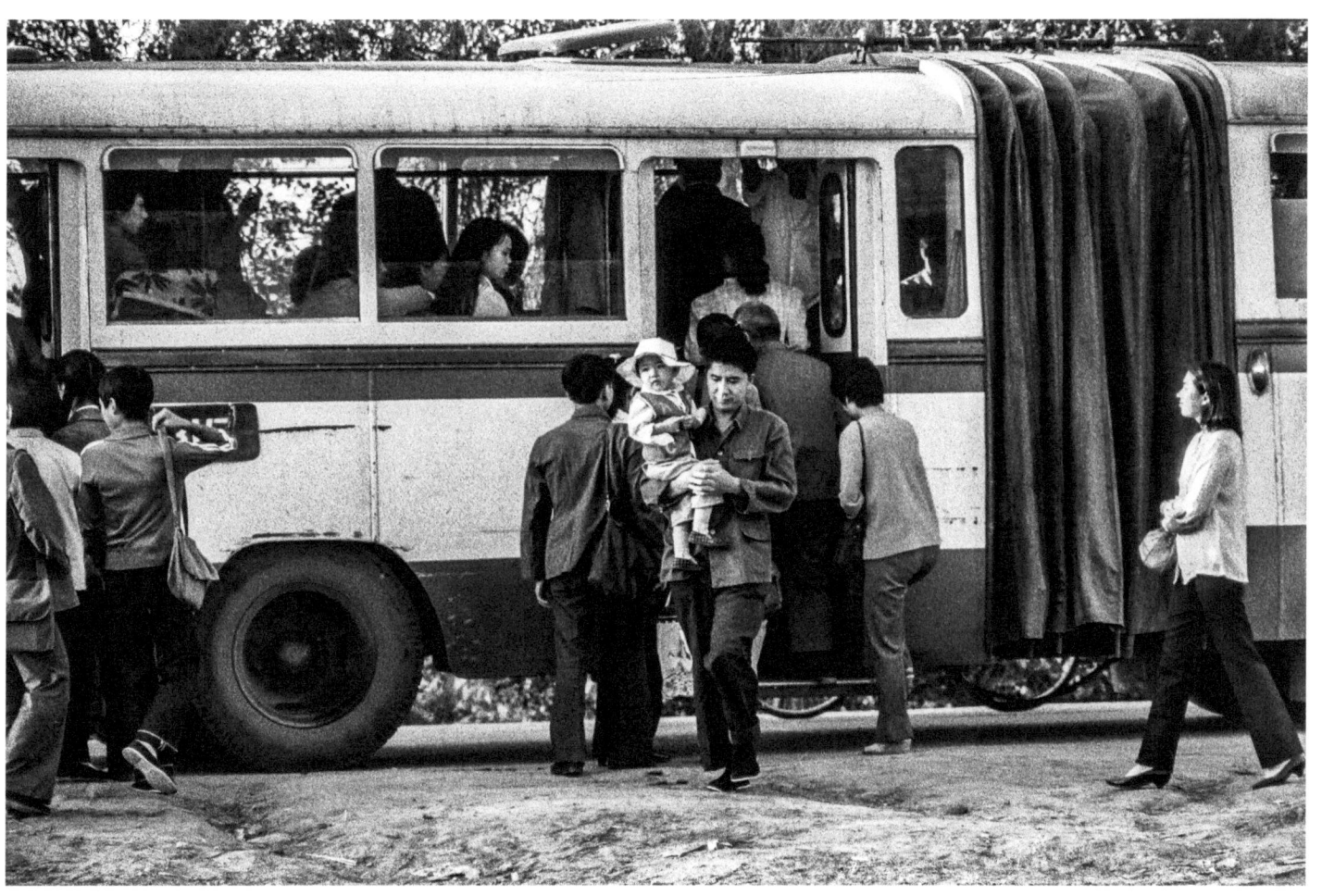

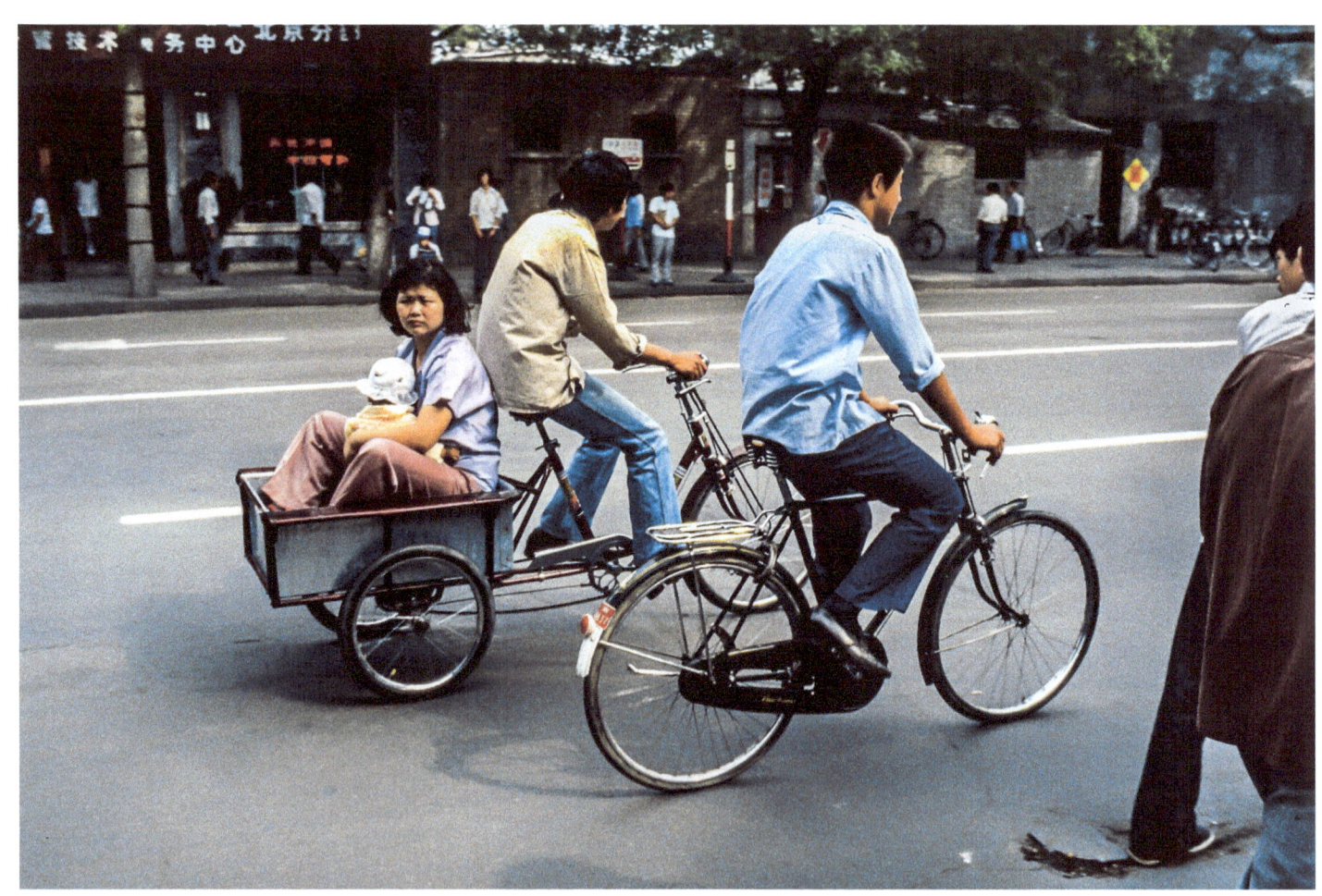

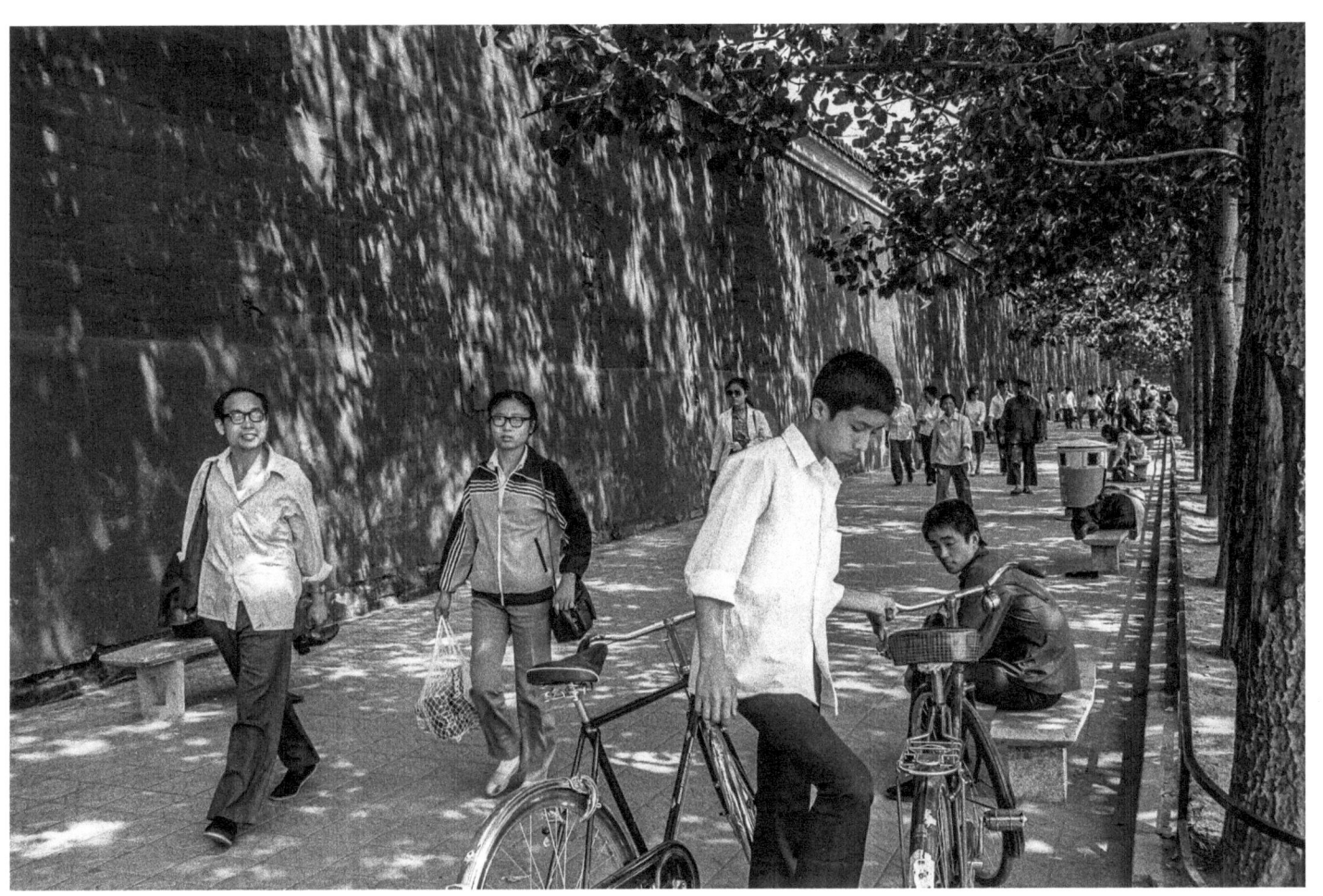

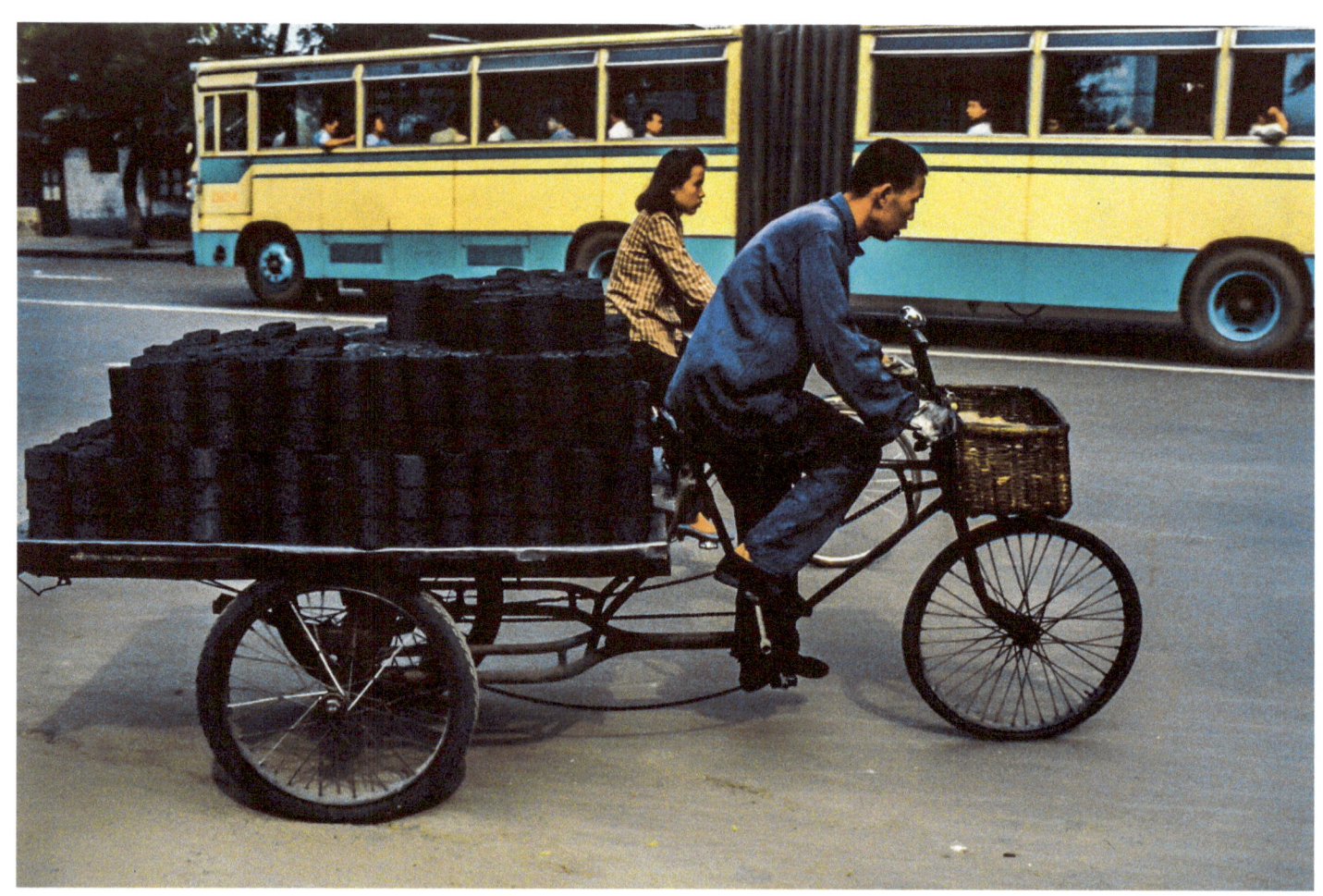

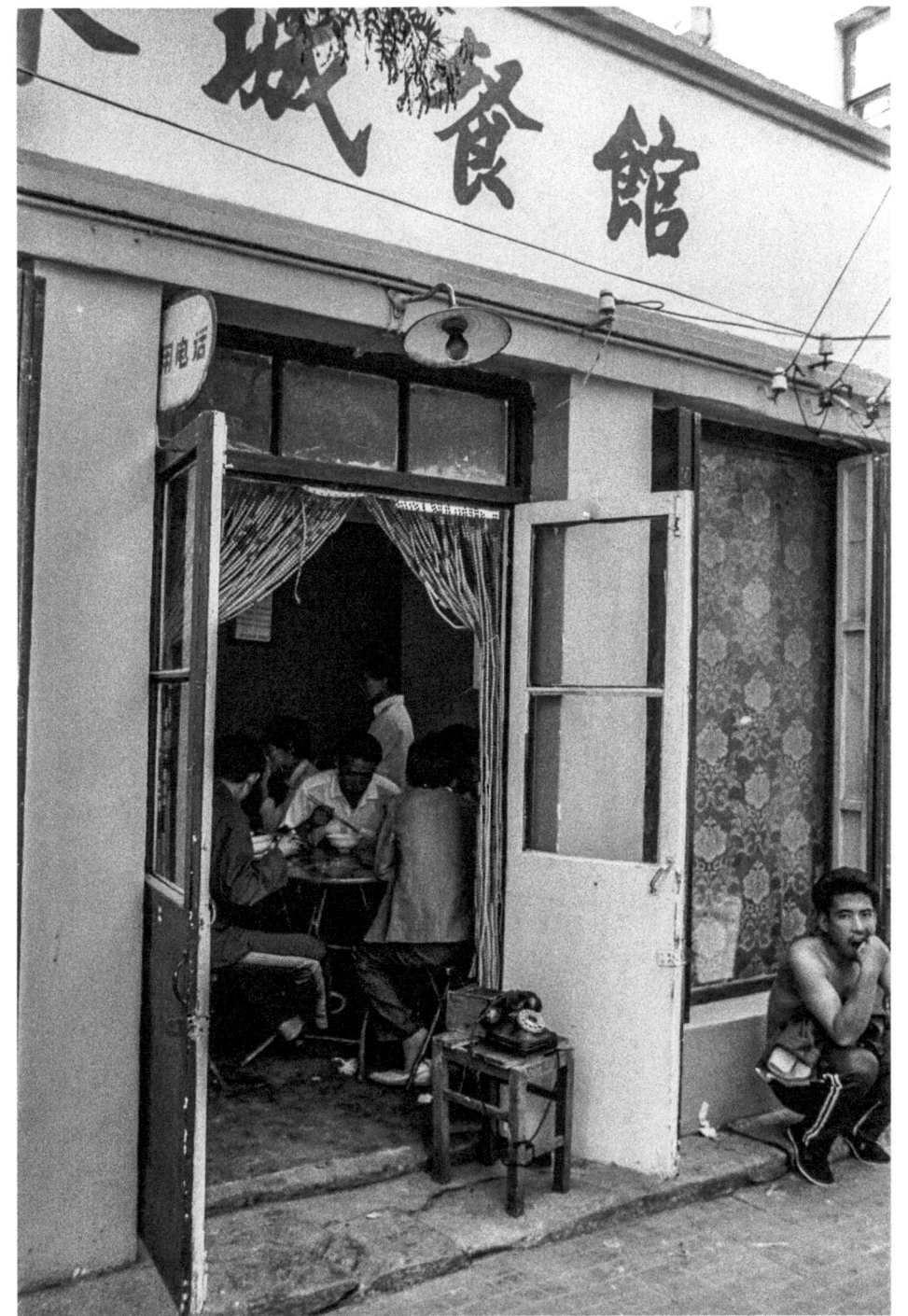

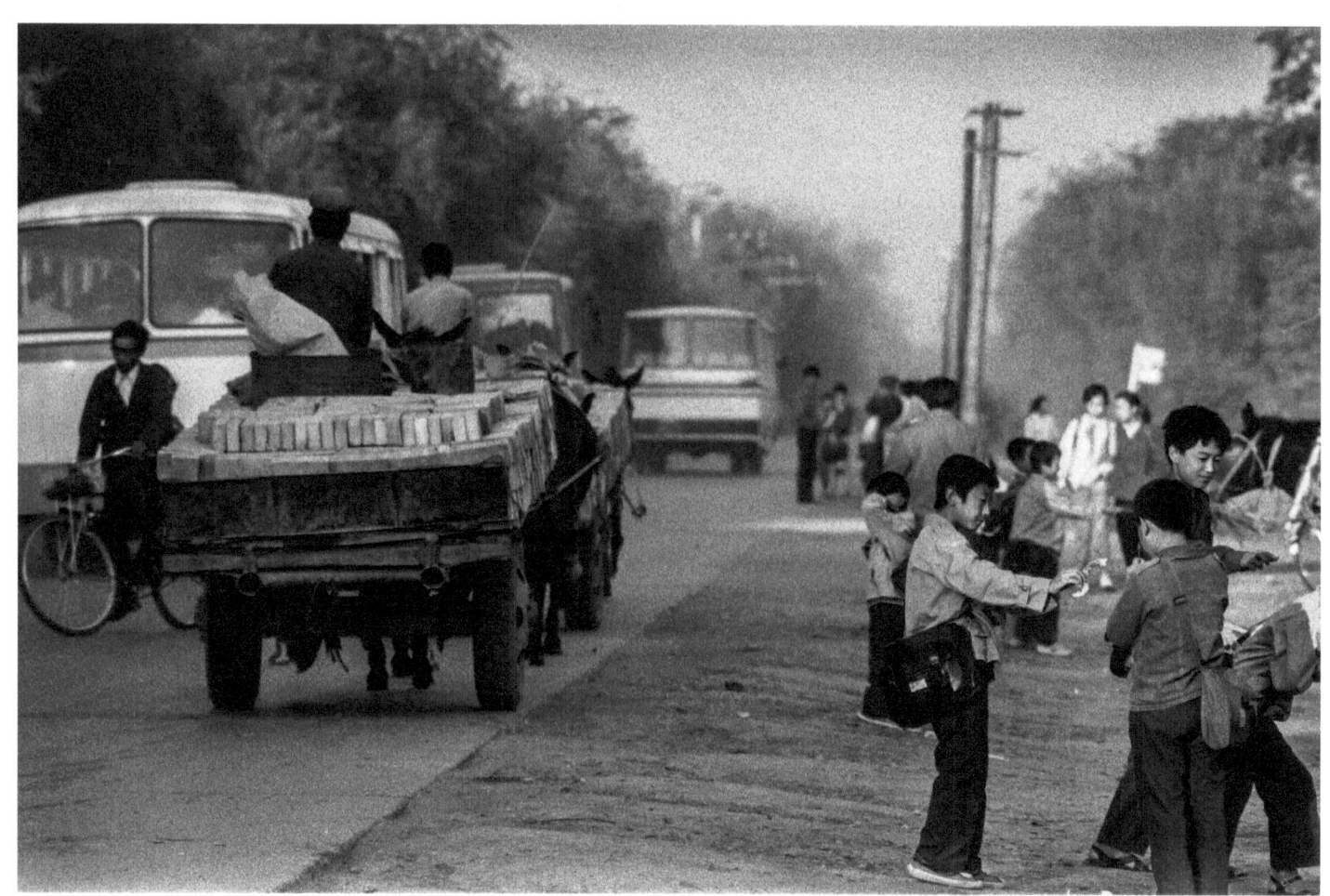

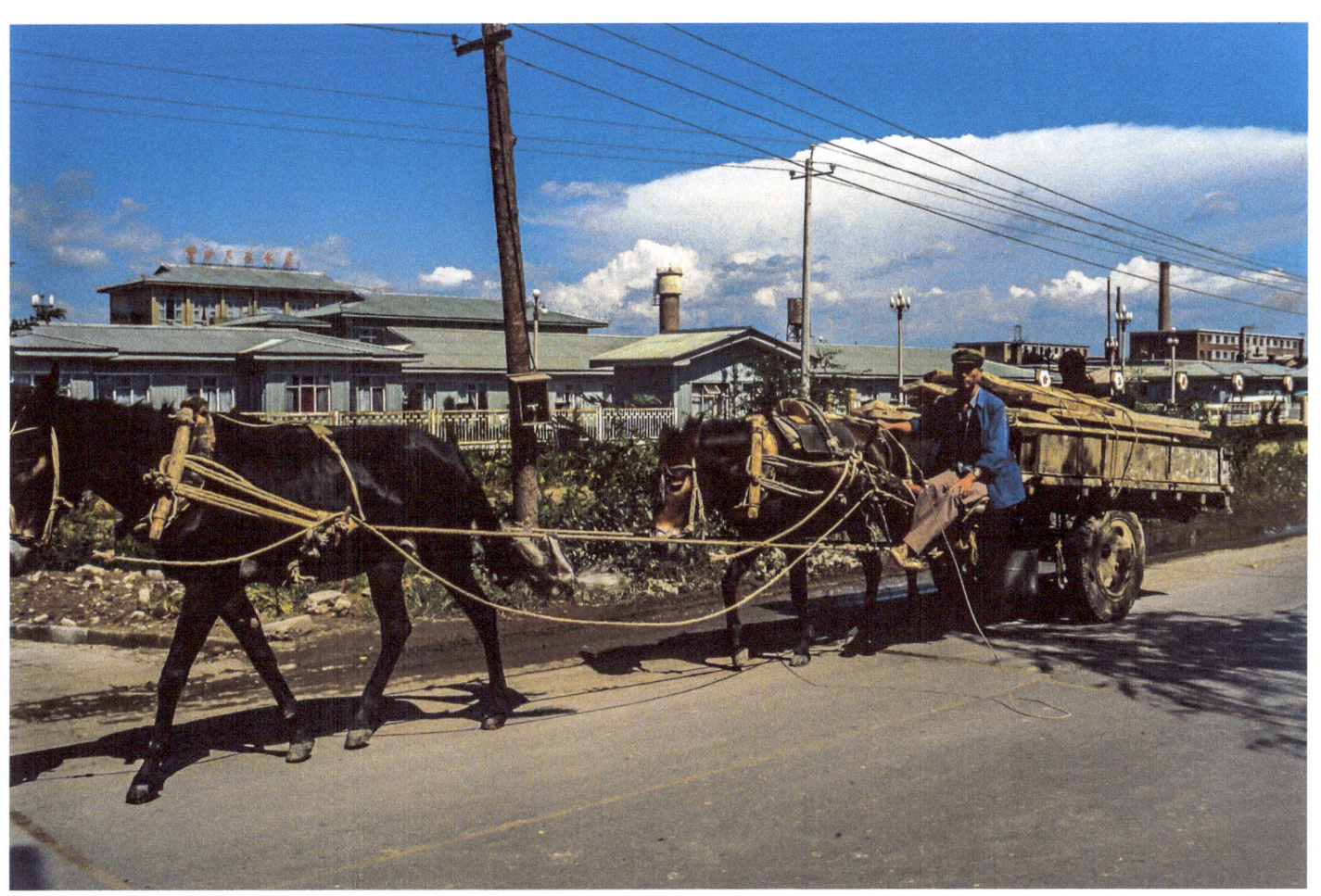

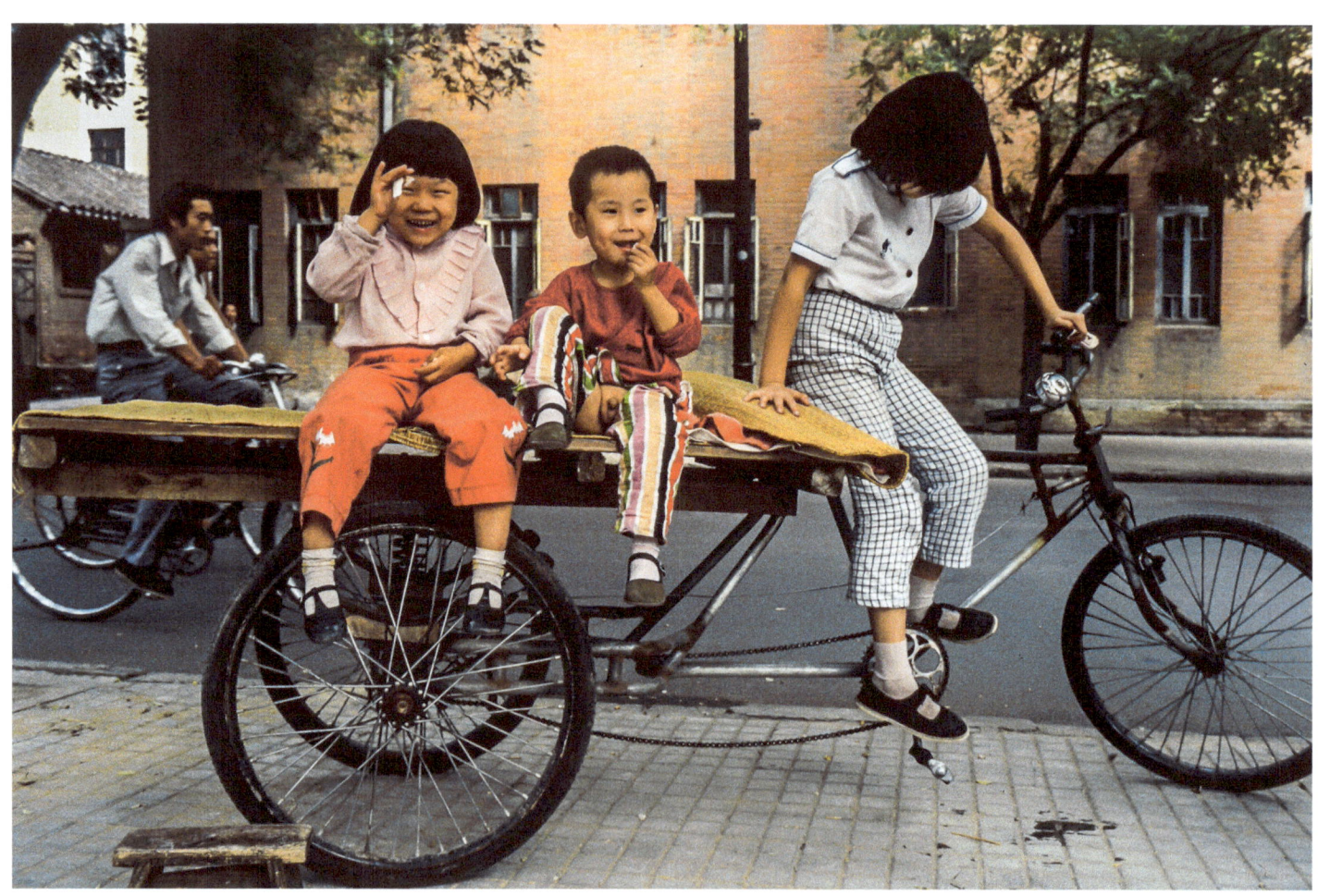

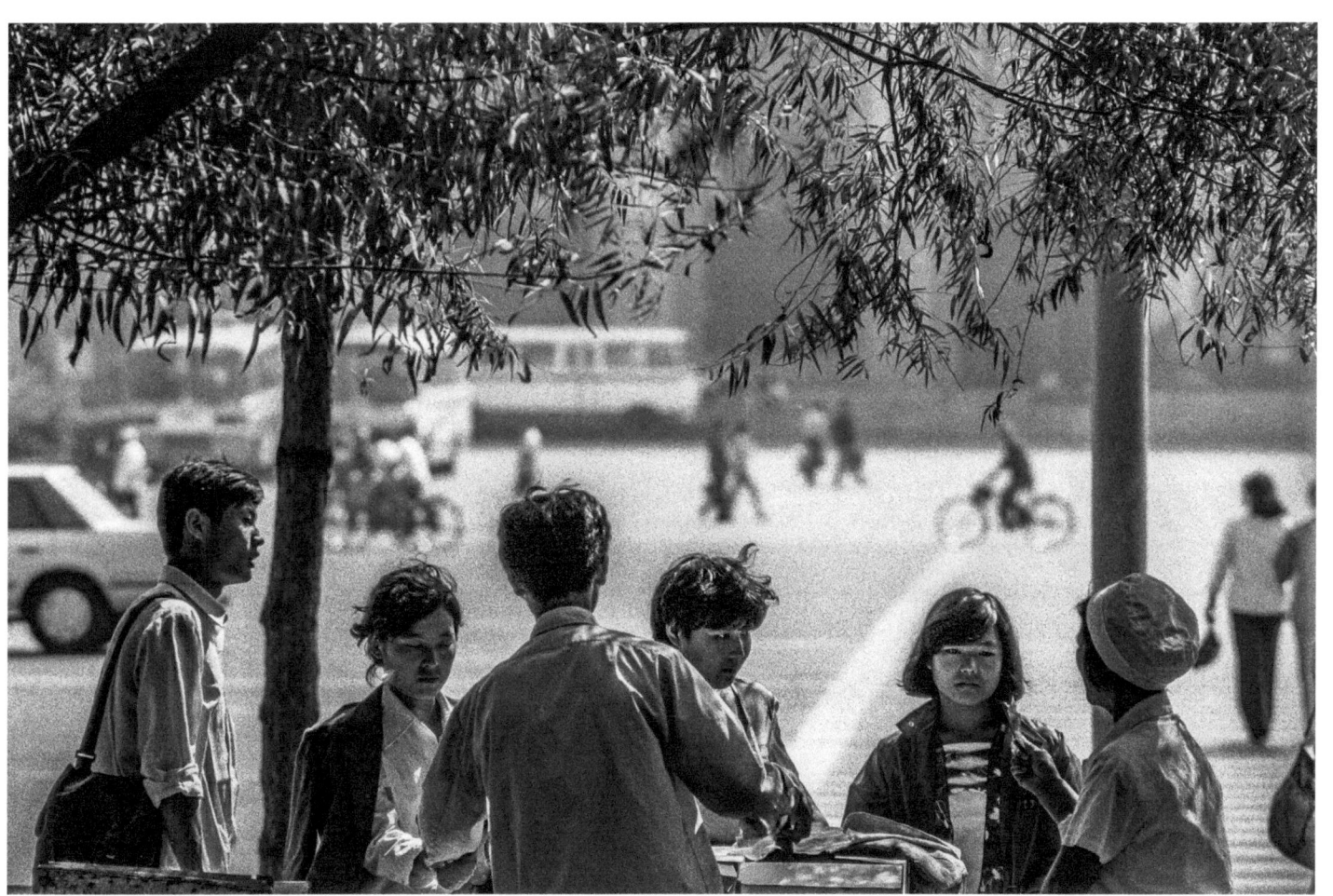

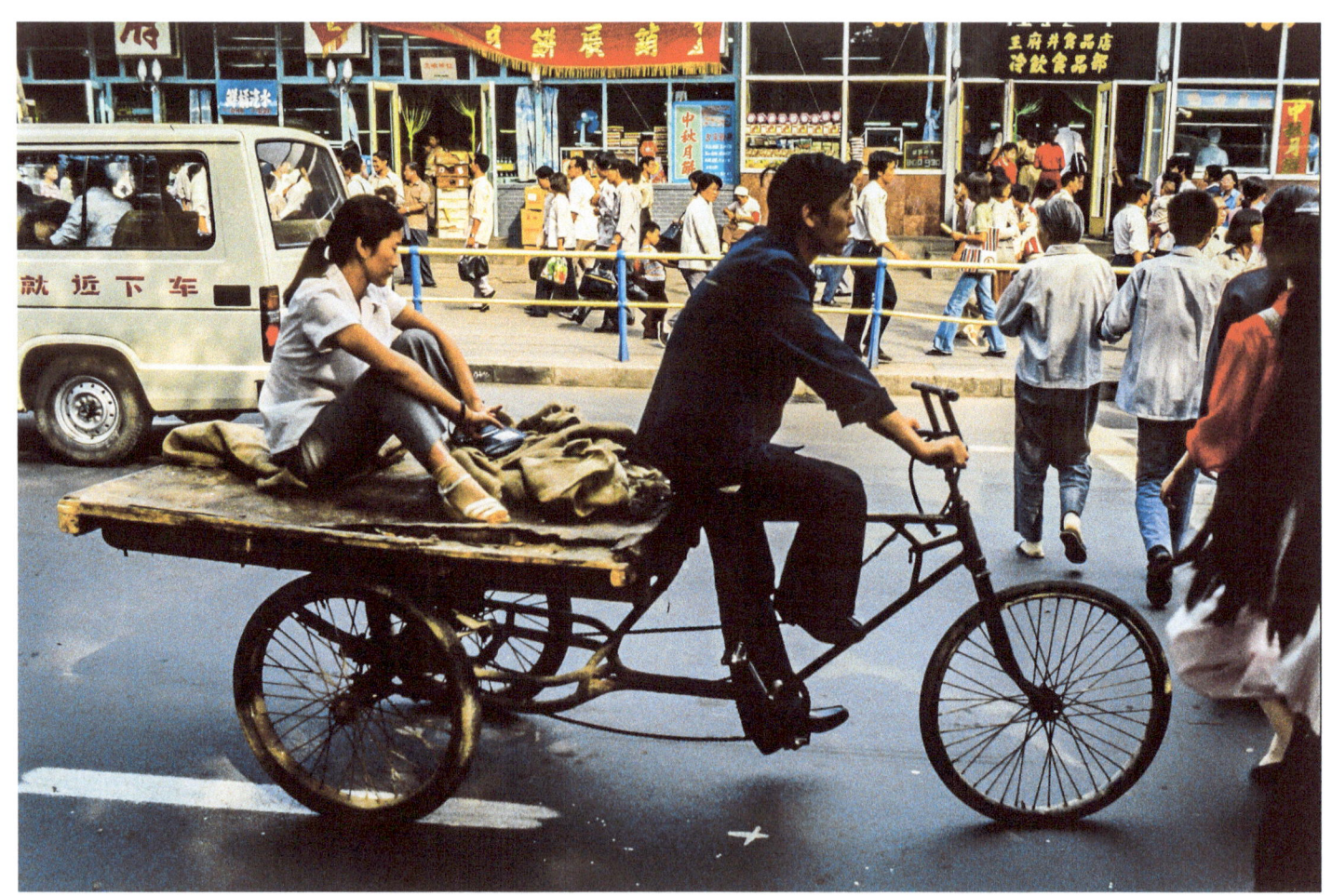

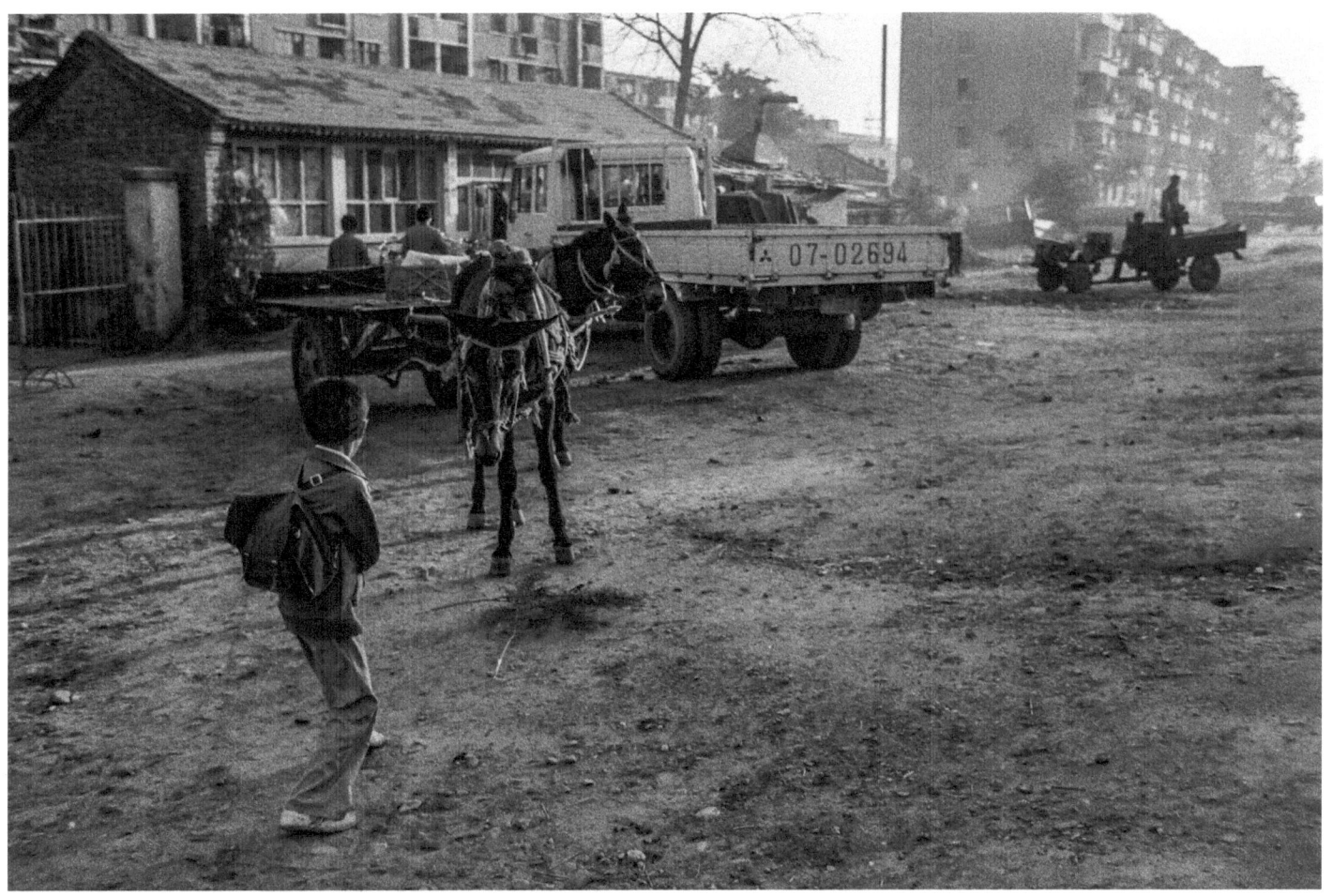

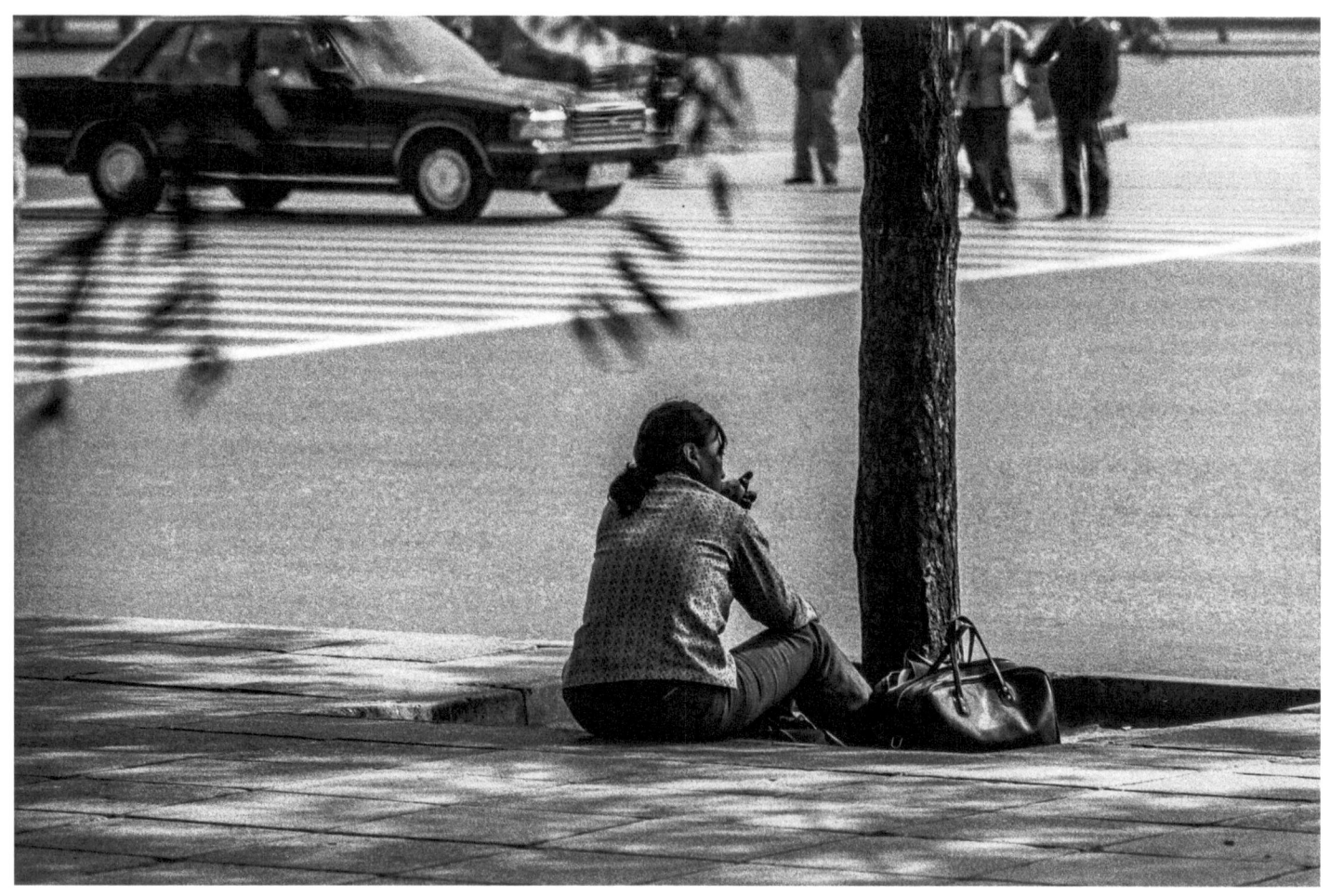

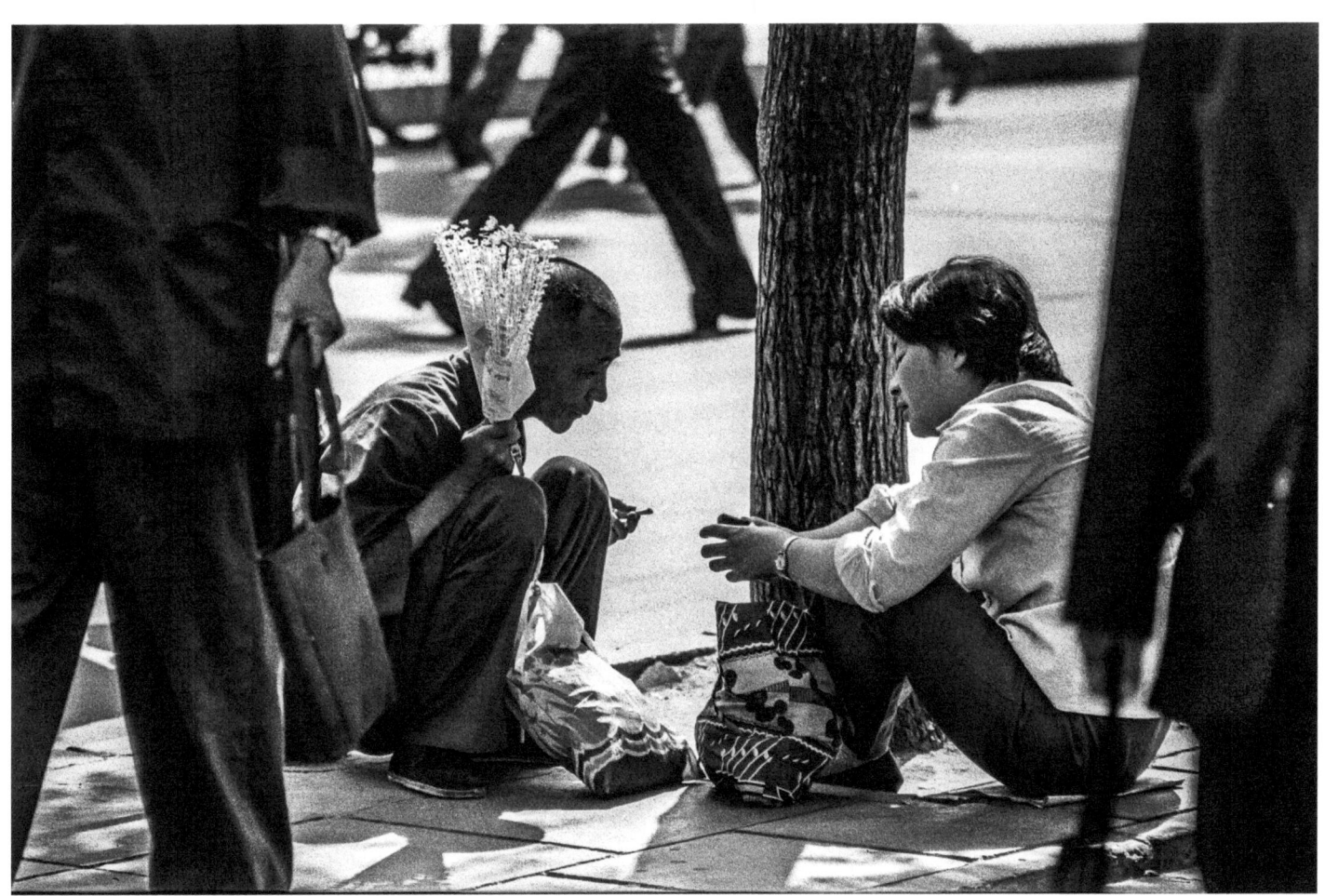

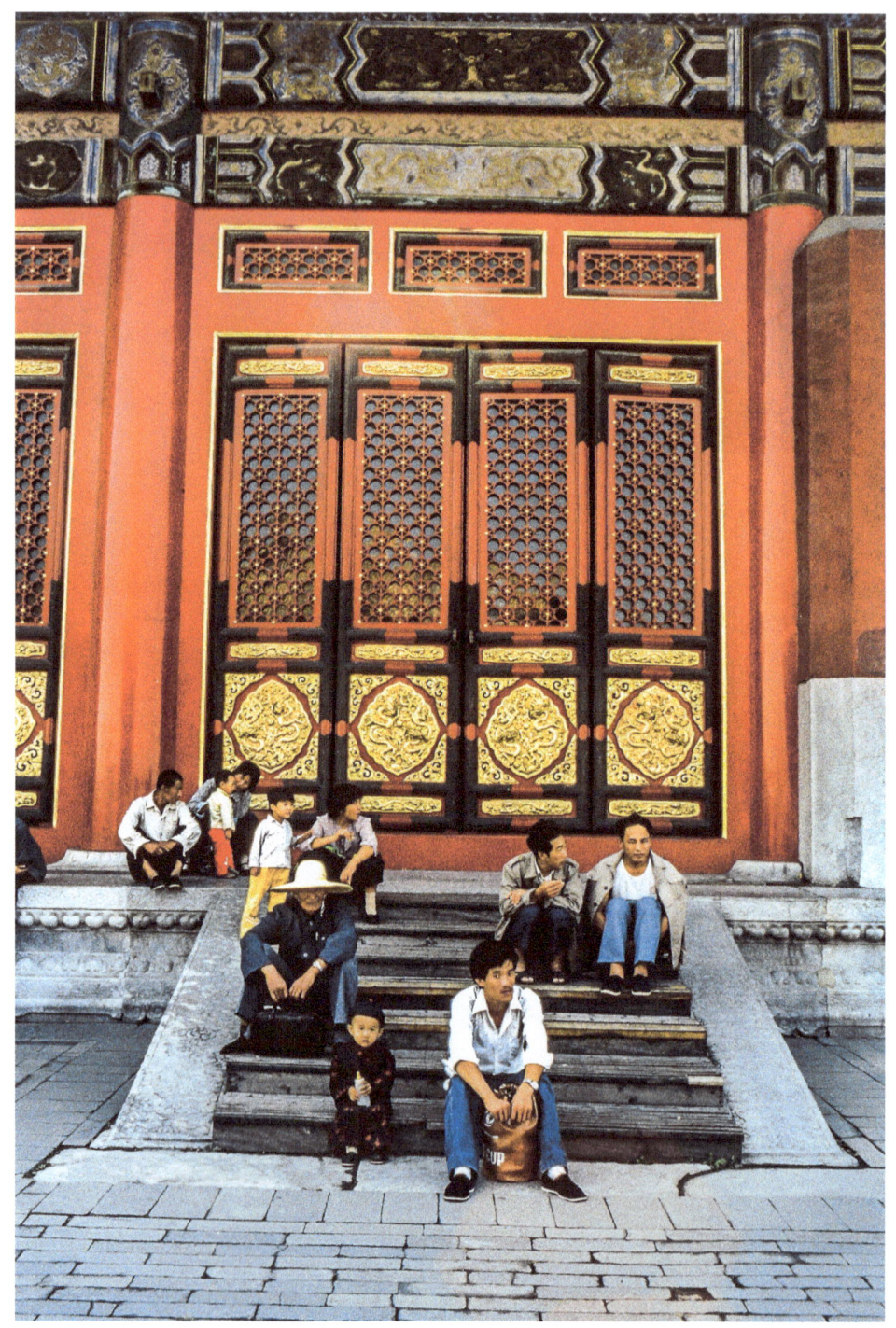

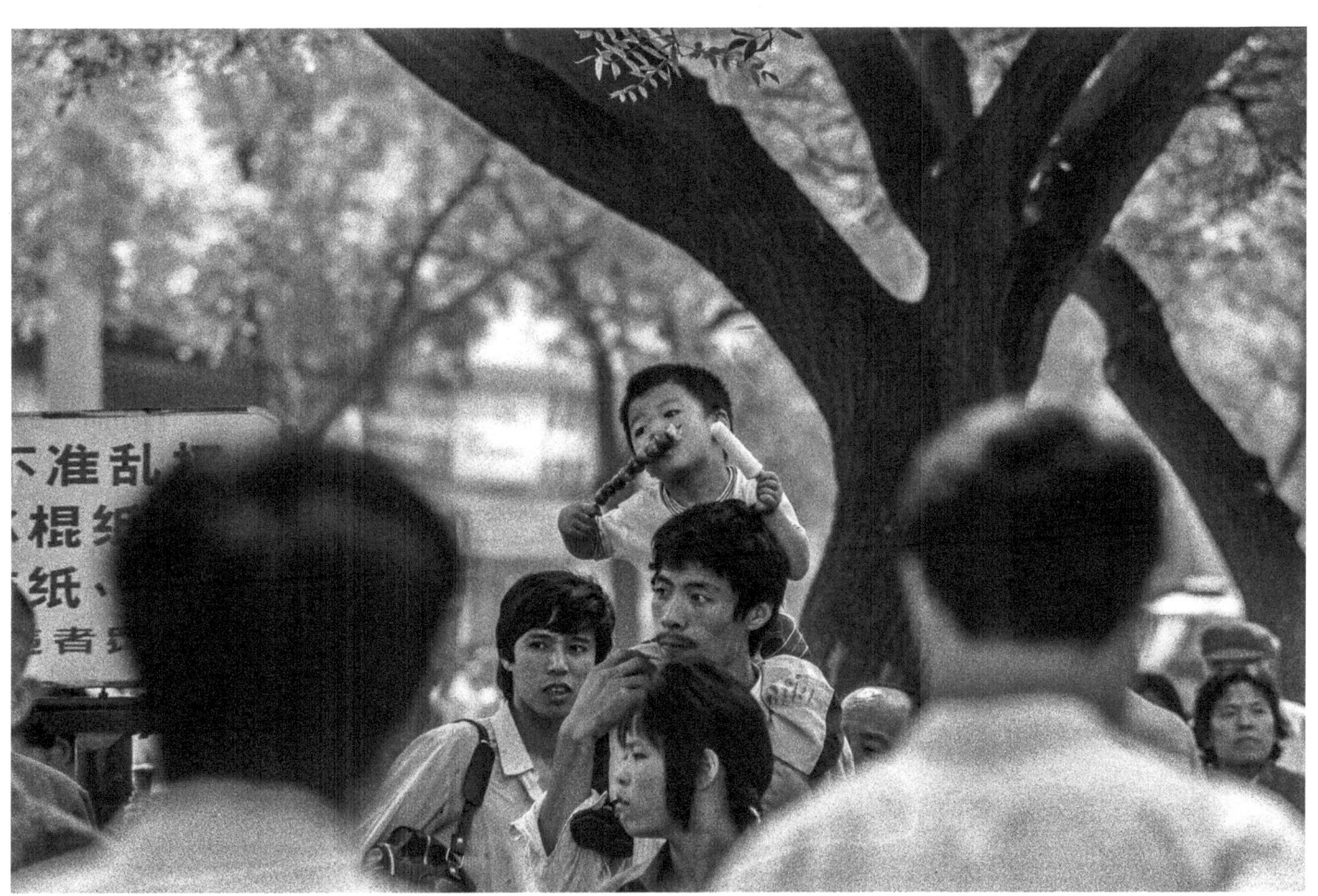

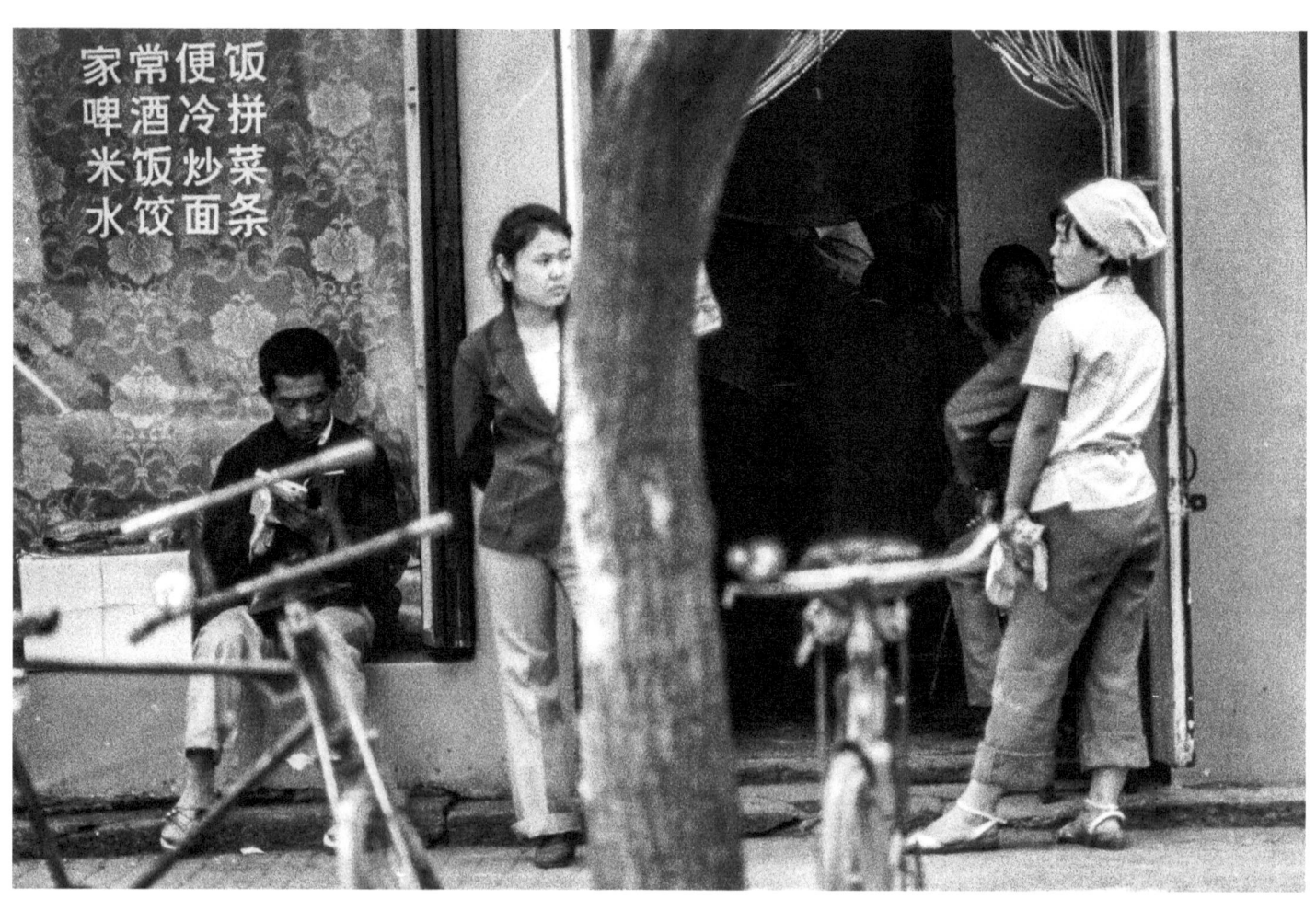

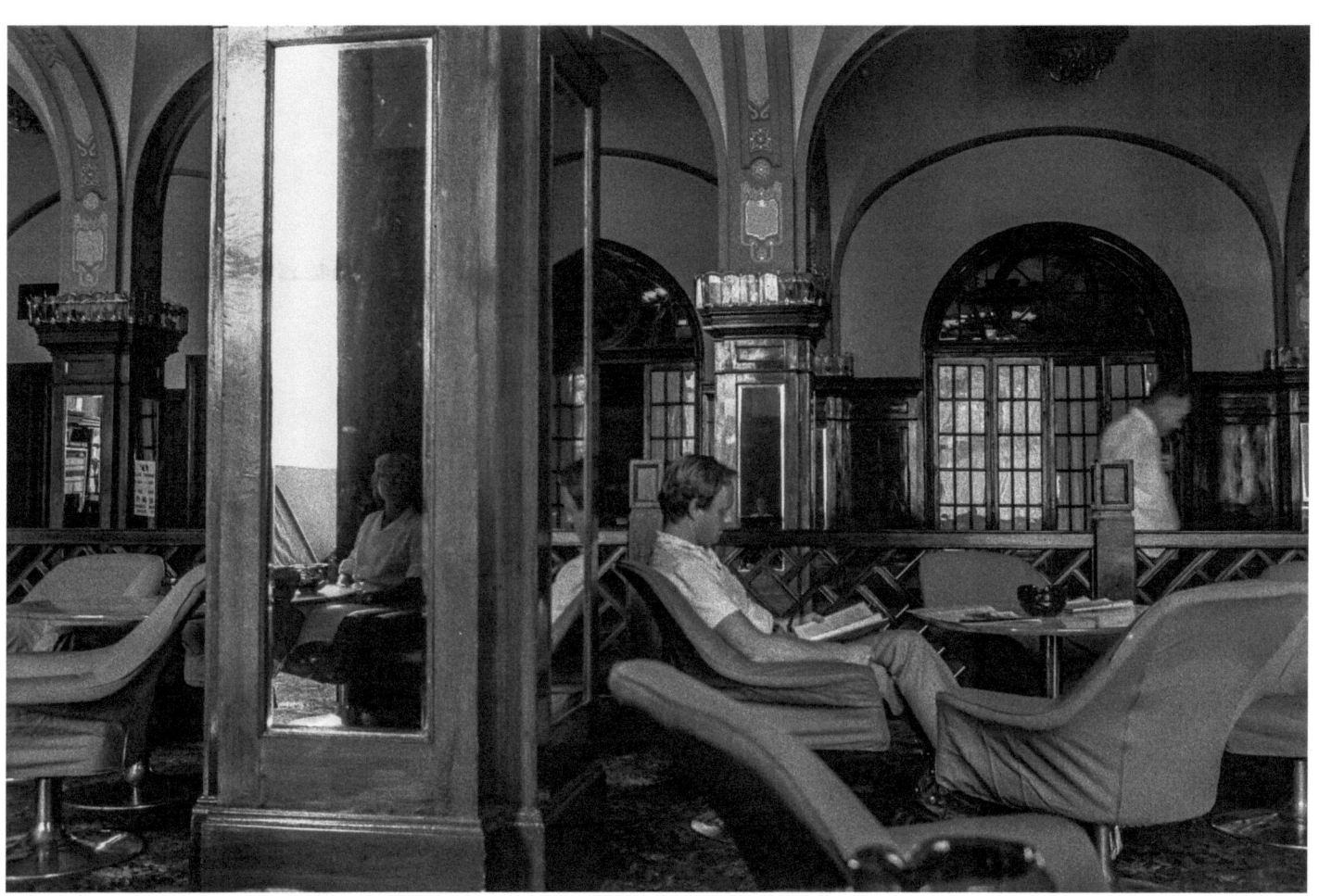

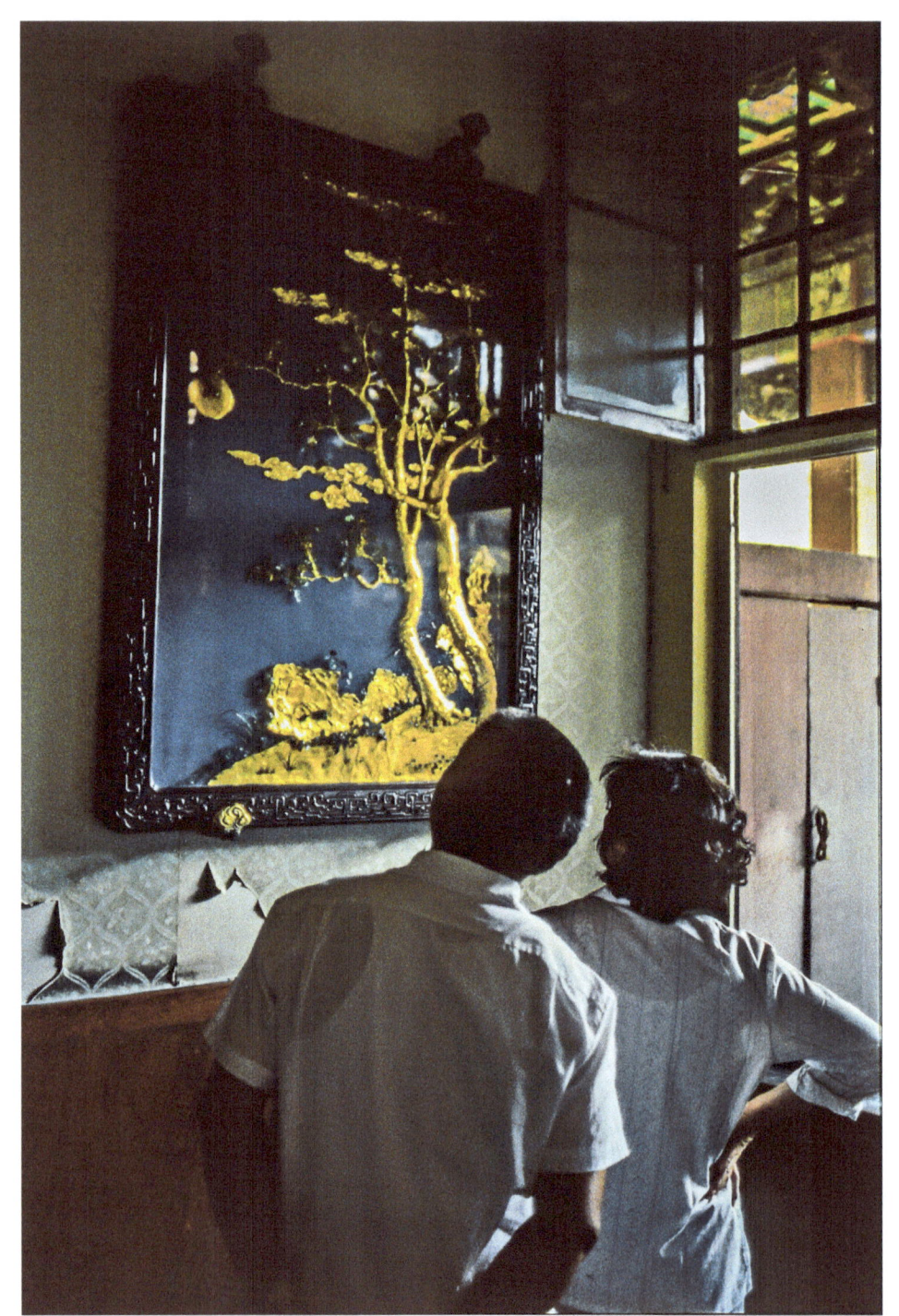

Bob in photography

Bob has been a photographer since the middle of last century. He started with an Agfa Isolette and was already the 15-year-old freelance photographer at the local newspaper Corren and Östgöten. He got a picture explained best football image of the magazine Match 1958. His work as a freelance photographer aroused interest in documentary photography, which has followed Bob through life.

He has photographed people, environments and nature on all seven continents. Today, Bob is professor emeritus at the University of Lund and is a photographer full time. Bob has had solo photo exhibitions at the Östergötland County Museum and in several other galleries.

Bovin Design Hb has published the following books:

New York remains. ISBN 978-1-4092-0178-6
En skola 1959. ISBN 978-91-978005-0-1
En skola 1959. e-book. ISBN 978-91-978005-1-8
Vårt skräp - framtidens fossil. e-book. ISBN 978-91-978005-2-5
Signs in situations. ISBN 978-91-978005-3-2
Humor i bilder. ISBN 978-91-978005-4-9
Humor i bilder. e-book. ISBN 978-91-978005-5-6
The Berlin Wall Falls. ISBN 978-91-978005-6-3
Berlinmurens fall. e-book. ISBN 978-91-978005-7-0
London 1967. A Photo Esaay. e-book. ISBN 978-91-978005-8-7
London 1967. A Photo Esaay. ISBN 978-91-978005-9-4
iStreetPhoto. ISBN 978-91-981019-1-1
iStreetPhoto. e-book. ISBN 978-91-981019-0-4

www.ingramcontent.com/pod-product-compliance
Lightning Source LLC
Chambersburg PA
CBHW051200220526
45473CB00003B/844